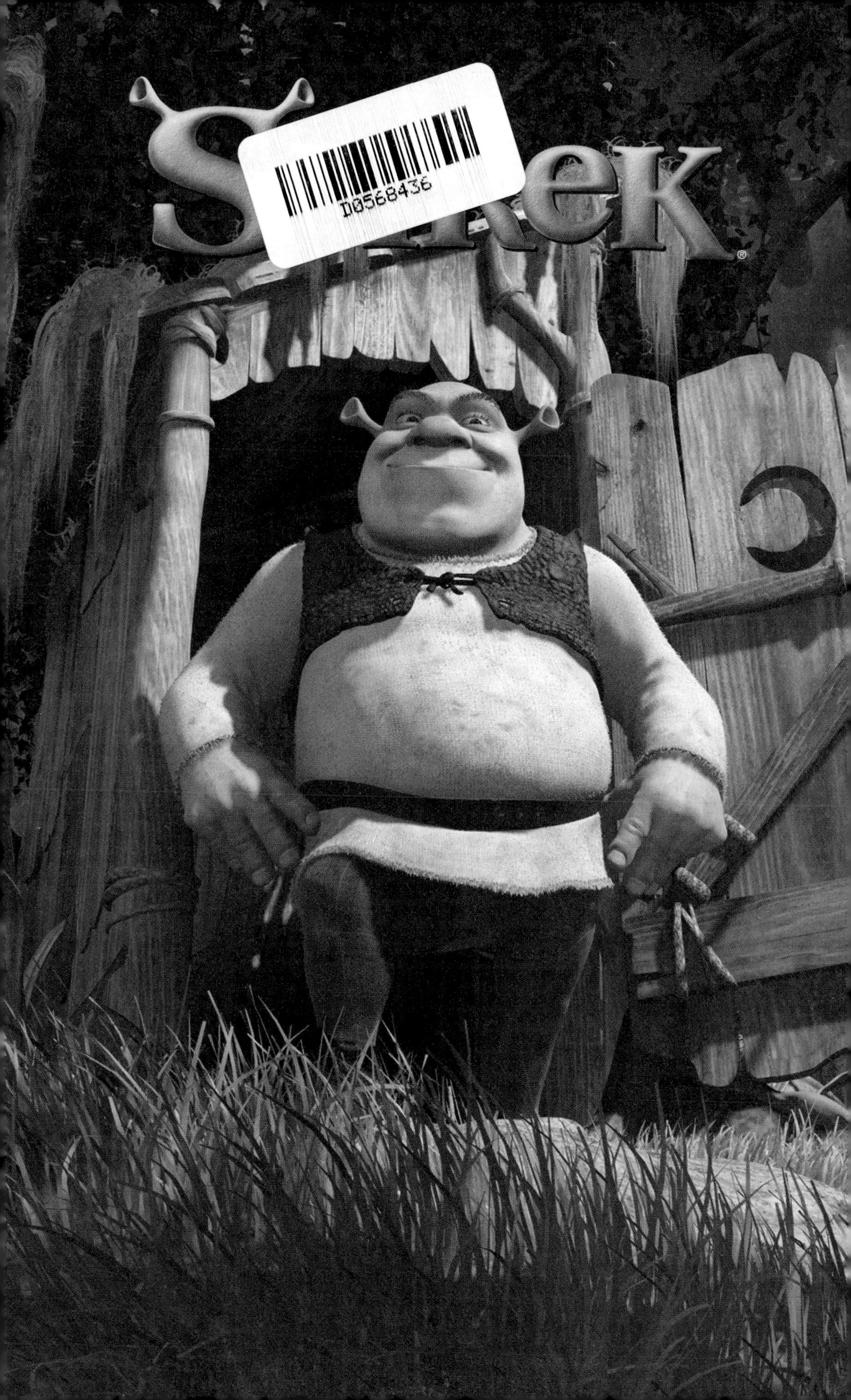

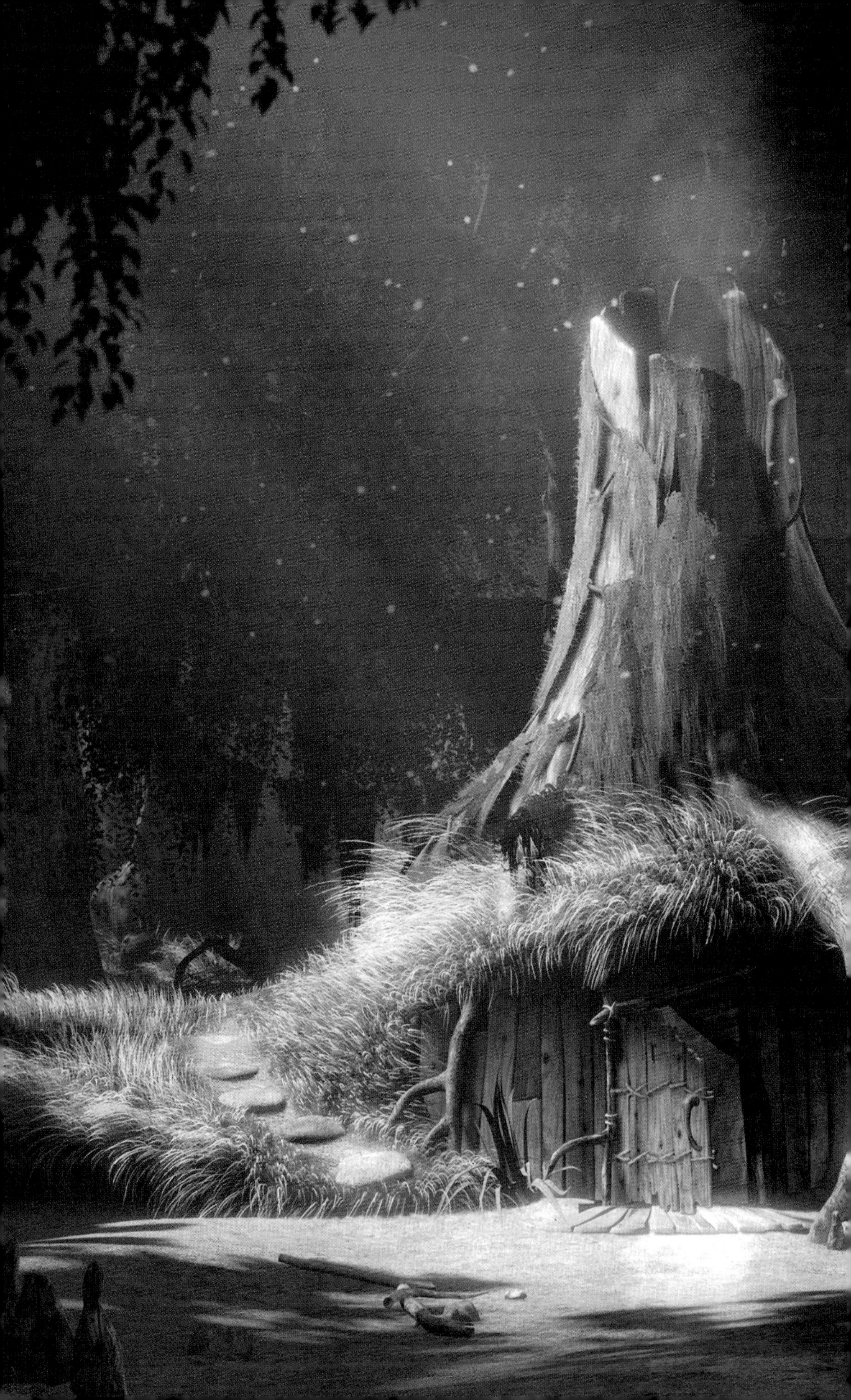

SHREK®

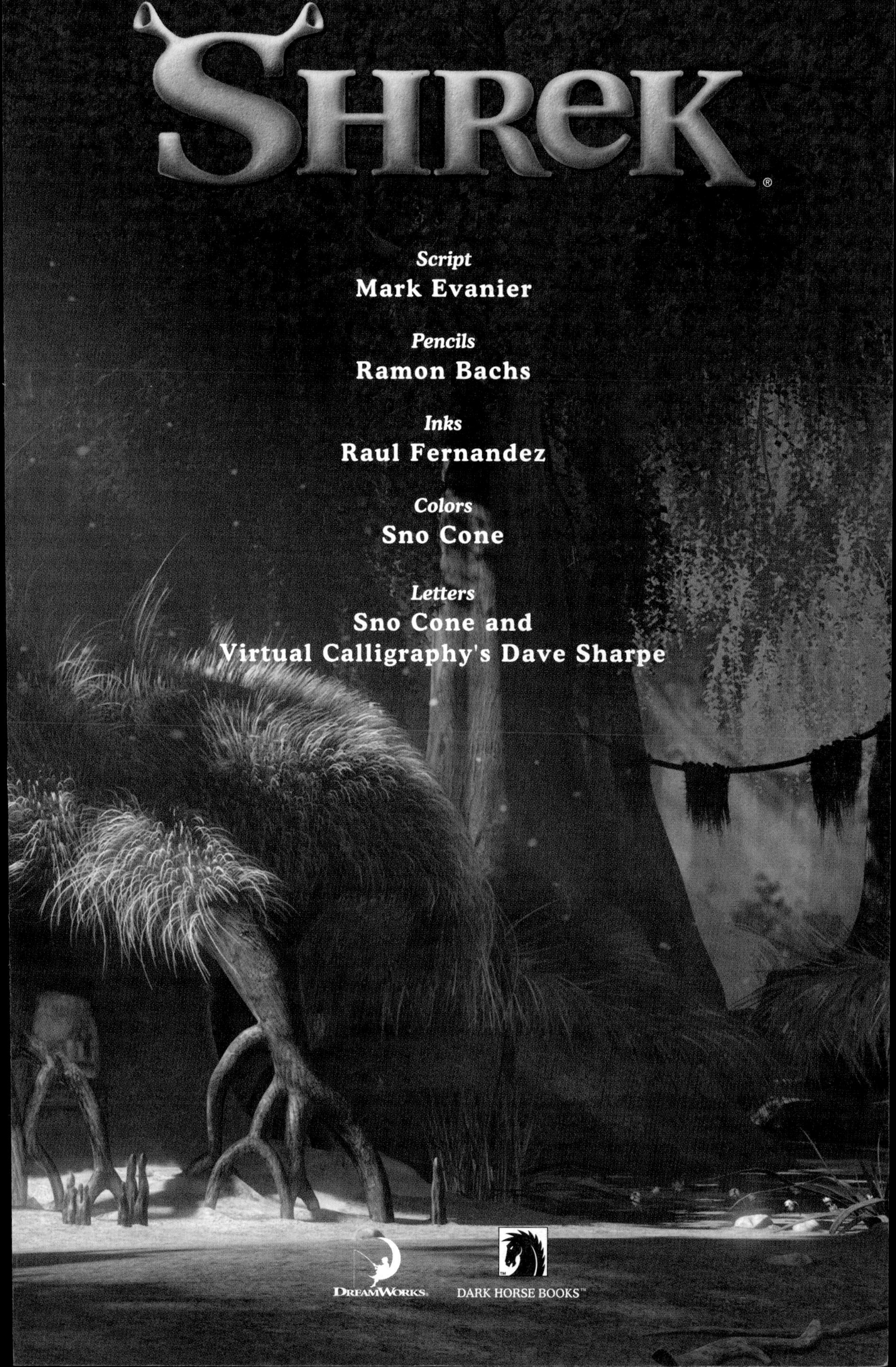

Script
Mark Evanier

Pencils
Ramon Bachs

Inks
Raul Fernandez

Colors
Sno Cone

Letters
Sno Cone and
Virtual Calligraphy's Dave Sharpe

DREAMWORKS DARK HORSE BOOKS™

Publisher
Mike Richardson

Editor
Dave Land

Editorial Assistant
Katie Moody

Collection Designer
Debra Bailey

This book collects issues 1 through 3 of the
Dark Horse comic-book series *Shrek*®

Dark Horse Books
A division of Dark Horse Comics, Inc.
10956 SE Main Street
Milwaukie, OR 97222

www.darkhorse.com

To find a comics shop in your area call the
Comic Shop Locator Service toll-free at (888) 266-4226

First edition: December 2003
ISBN: 1-56971-982-9

3 5 7 9 10 8 6 4 2

Printed in Canada

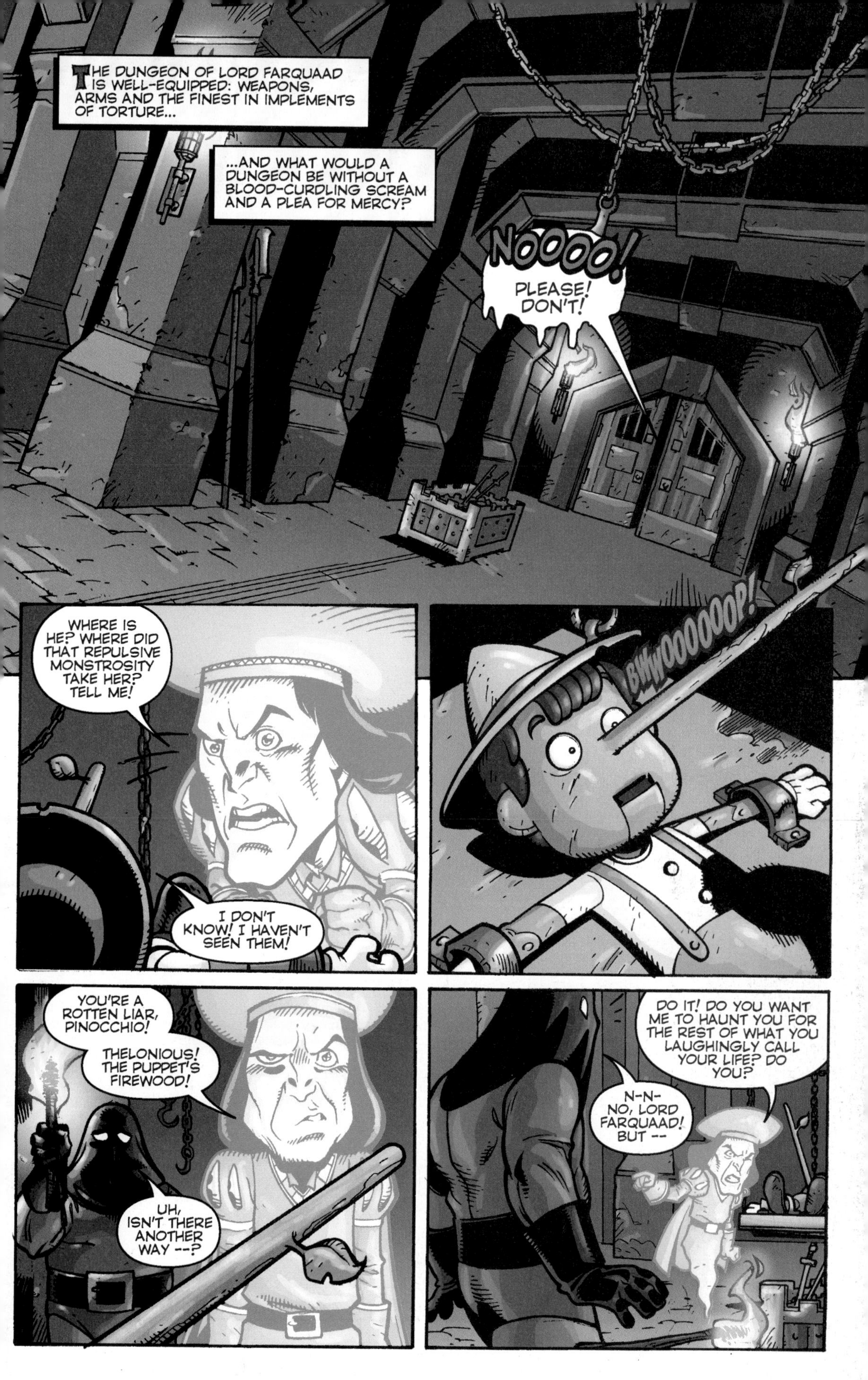
THE DUNGEON OF LORD FARQUAAD IS WELL-EQUIPPED: WEAPONS, ARMS AND THE FINEST IN IMPLEMENTS OF TORTURE...
...AND WHAT WOULD A DUNGEON BE WITHOUT A BLOOD-CURDLING SCREAM AND A PLEA FOR MERCY?
NOOOO!
PLEASE! DON'T!
WHERE IS HE? WHERE DID THAT REPULSIVE MONSTROSITY TAKE HER? TELL ME!
I DON'T KNOW! I HAVEN'T SEEN THEM!
BWWOOOOOOP!
YOU'RE A ROTTEN LIAR, PINOCCHIO!
THELONIOUS! THE PUPPET'S FIREWOOD!
UH, ISN'T THERE ANOTHER WAY --?
DO IT! DO YOU WANT ME TO HAUNT YOU FOR THE REST OF WHAT YOU LAUGHINGLY CALL YOUR LIFE? DO YOU?
N-N-NO, LORD FARQUAAD! BUT --

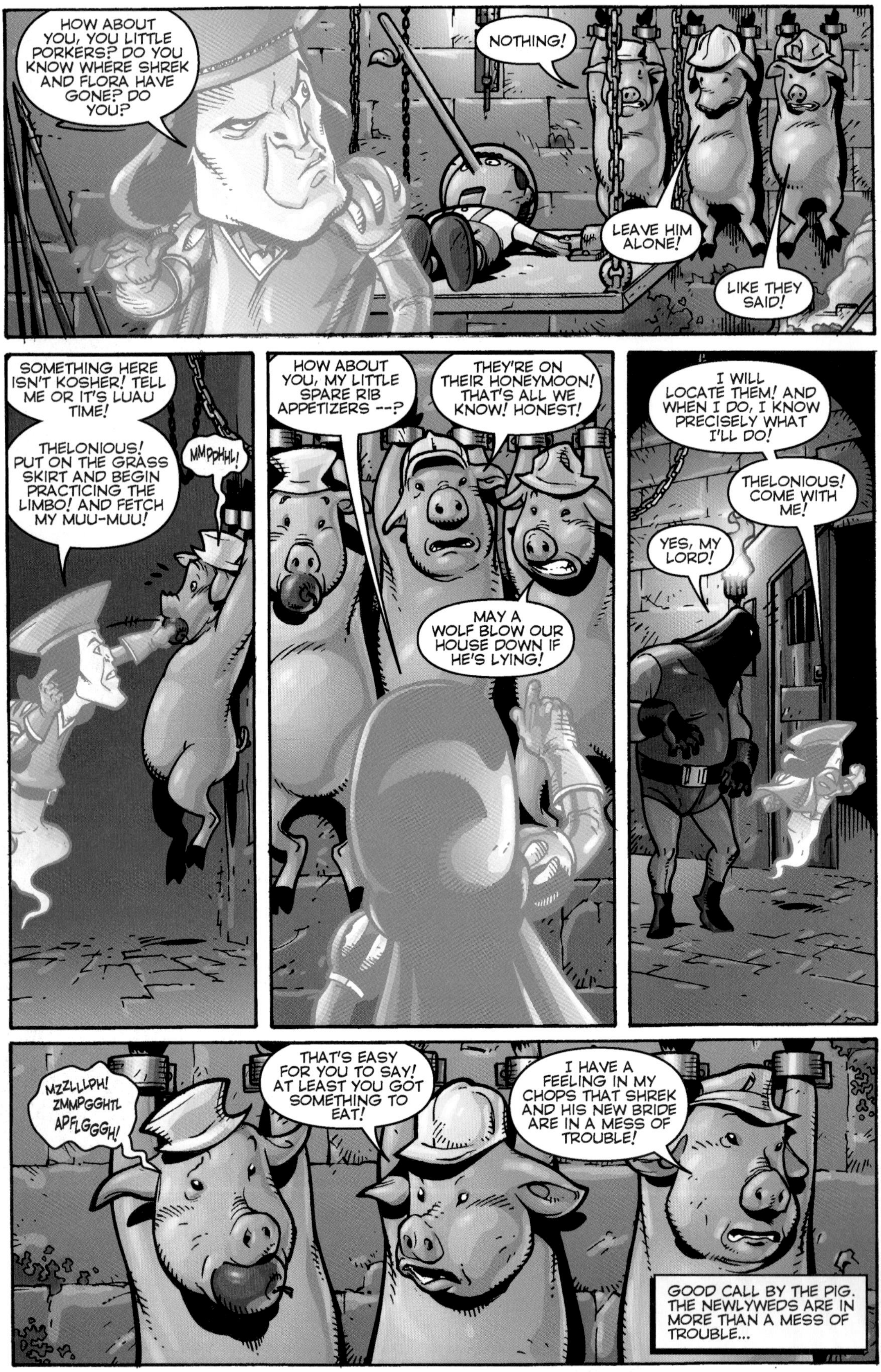

HOW ABOUT YOU, YOU LITTLE PORKERS? DO YOU KNOW WHERE SHREK AND FLORA HAVE GONE? DO YOU?
NOTHING!
LEAVE HIM ALONE!
LIKE THEY SAID!
SOMETHING HERE ISN'T KOSHER! TELL ME OR IT'S LUAU TIME!
THELONIOUS! PUT ON THE GRASS SKIRT AND BEGIN PRACTICING THE LIMBO! AND FETCH MY MUU-MUU!
MMPPHHL!
HOW ABOUT YOU, MY LITTLE SPARE RIB APPETIZERS --?
THEY'RE ON THEIR HONEYMOON! THAT'S ALL WE KNOW! HONEST!
MAY A WOLF BLOW OUR HOUSE DOWN IF HE'S LYING!
I WILL LOCATE THEM! AND WHEN I DO, I KNOW PRECISELY WHAT I'LL DO!
THELONIOUS! COME WITH ME!
YES, MY LORD!
MZZLLLPH! ZMMPGGHTL APFLGGGH!
THAT'S EASY FOR YOU TO SAY! AT LEAST YOU GOT SOMETHING TO EAT!
I HAVE A FEELING IN MY CHOPS THAT SHREK AND HIS NEW BRIDE ARE IN A MESS OF TROUBLE!
GOOD CALL BY THE PIG. THE NEWLYWEDS ARE IN MORE THAN A MESS OF TROUBLE...

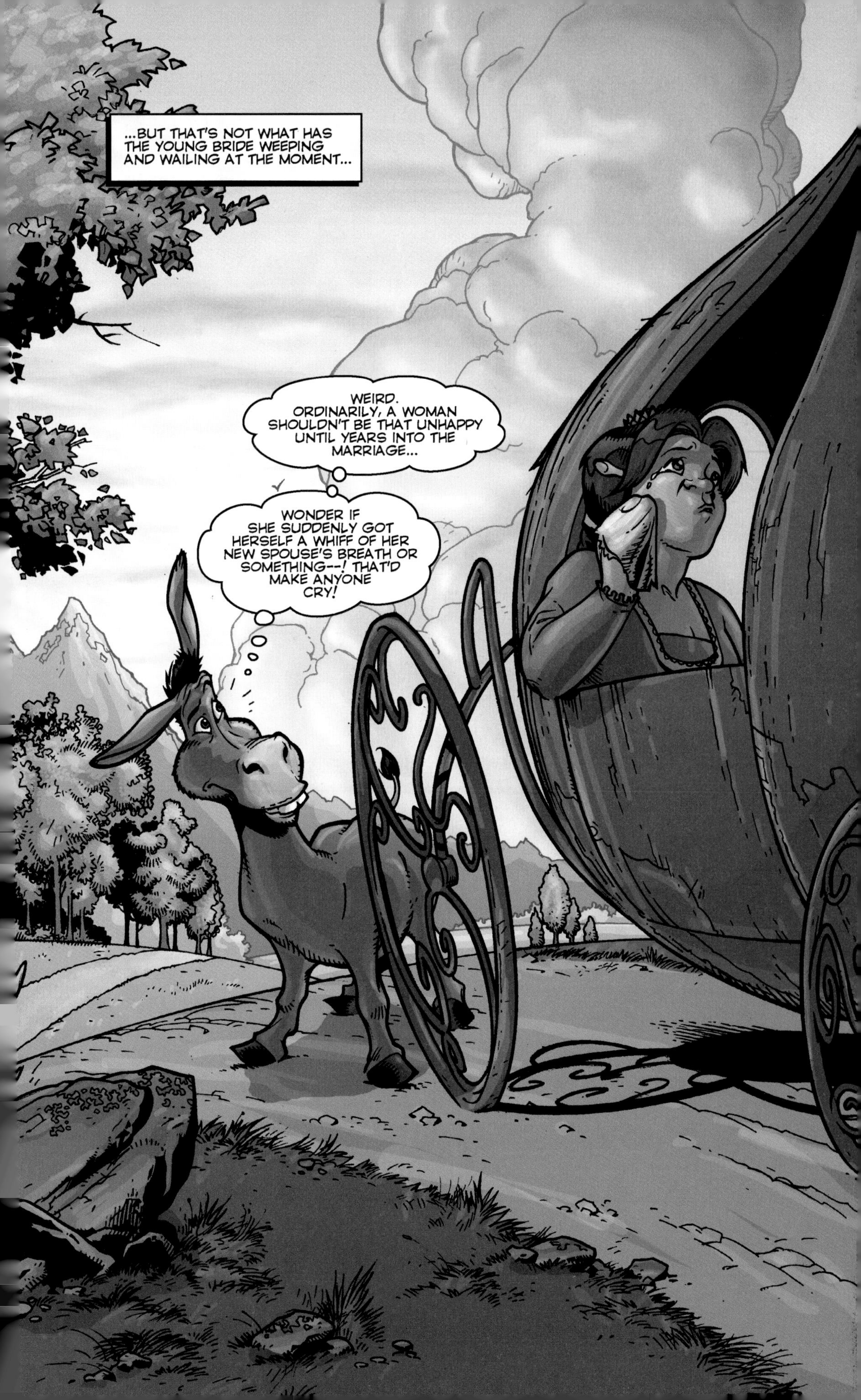
...BUT THAT'S NOT WHAT HAS THE YOUNG BRIDE WEEPING AND WAILING AT THE MOMENT...
WEIRD. ORDINARILY, A WOMAN SHOULDN'T BE THAT UNHAPPY UNTIL YEARS INTO THE MARRIAGE...
WONDER IF SHE SUDDENLY GOT HERSELF A WHIFF OF HER NEW SPOUSE'S BREATH OR SOMETHING--! THAT'D MAKE ANYONE CRY!

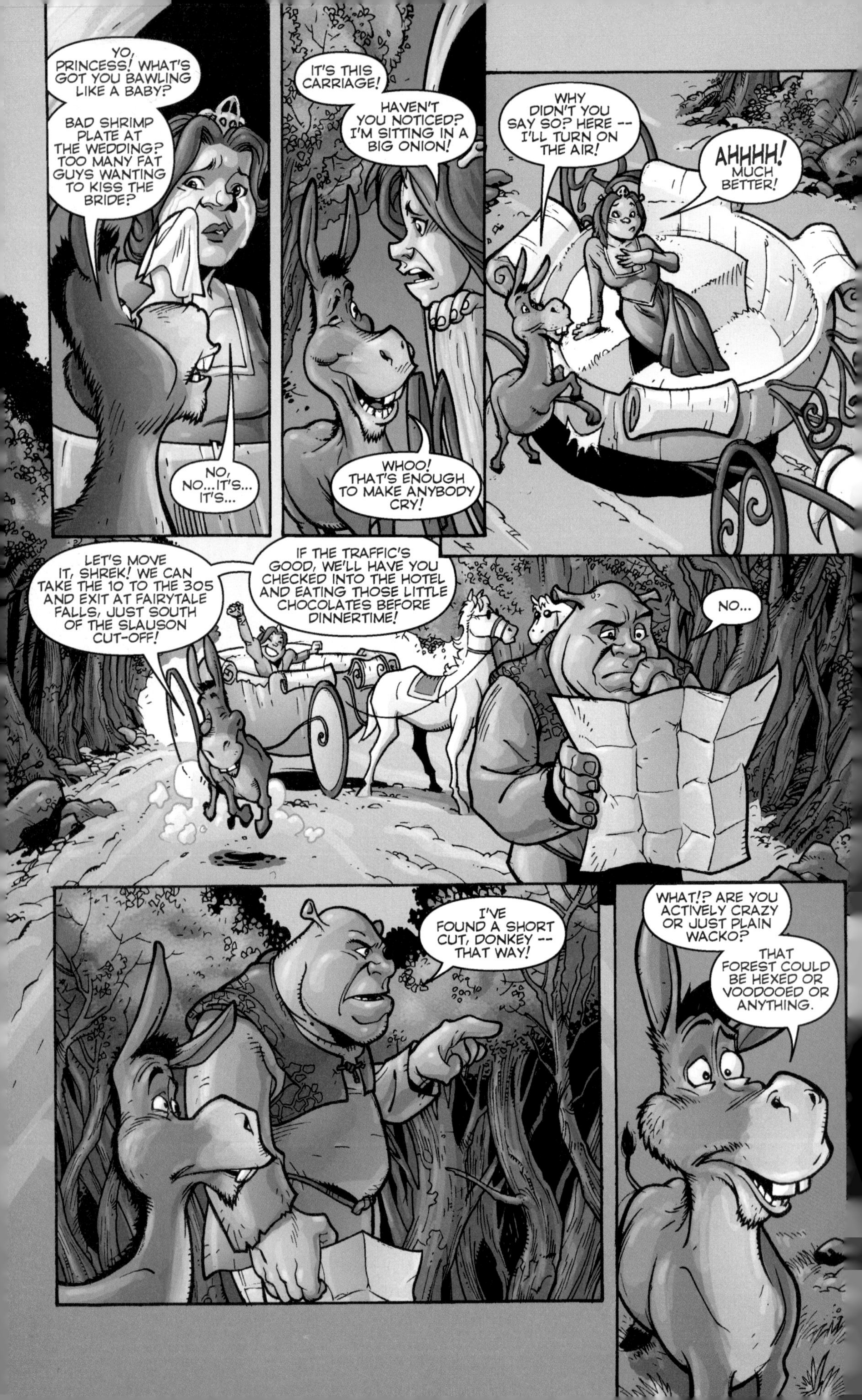
YO, PRINCESS! WHAT'S GOT YOU BAWLING LIKE A BABY?
BAD SHRIMP PLATE AT THE WEDDING? TOO MANY FAT GUYS WANTING TO KISS THE BRIDE?
NO, NO...IT'S... IT'S...
IT'S THIS CARRIAGE!
HAVEN'T YOU NOTICED? I'M SITTING IN A BIG ONION!
WHOO! THAT'S ENOUGH TO MAKE ANYBODY CRY!
WHY DIDN'T YOU SAY SO? HERE -- I'LL TURN ON THE AIR!
AHHHH! MUCH BETTER!
LET'S MOVE IT, SHREK! WE CAN TAKE THE 10 TO THE 305 AND EXIT AT FAIRYTALE FALLS, JUST SOUTH OF THE SLAUSON CUT-OFF!
IF THE TRAFFIC'S GOOD, WE'LL HAVE YOU CHECKED INTO THE HOTEL AND EATING THOSE LITTLE CHOCOLATES BEFORE DINNERTIME!
NO...
I'VE FOUND A SHORT CUT, DONKEY -- THAT WAY!
WHAT!? ARE YOU ACTIVELY CRAZY OR JUST PLAIN WACKO?
THAT FOREST COULD BE HEXED OR VOODOOED OR ANYTHING.

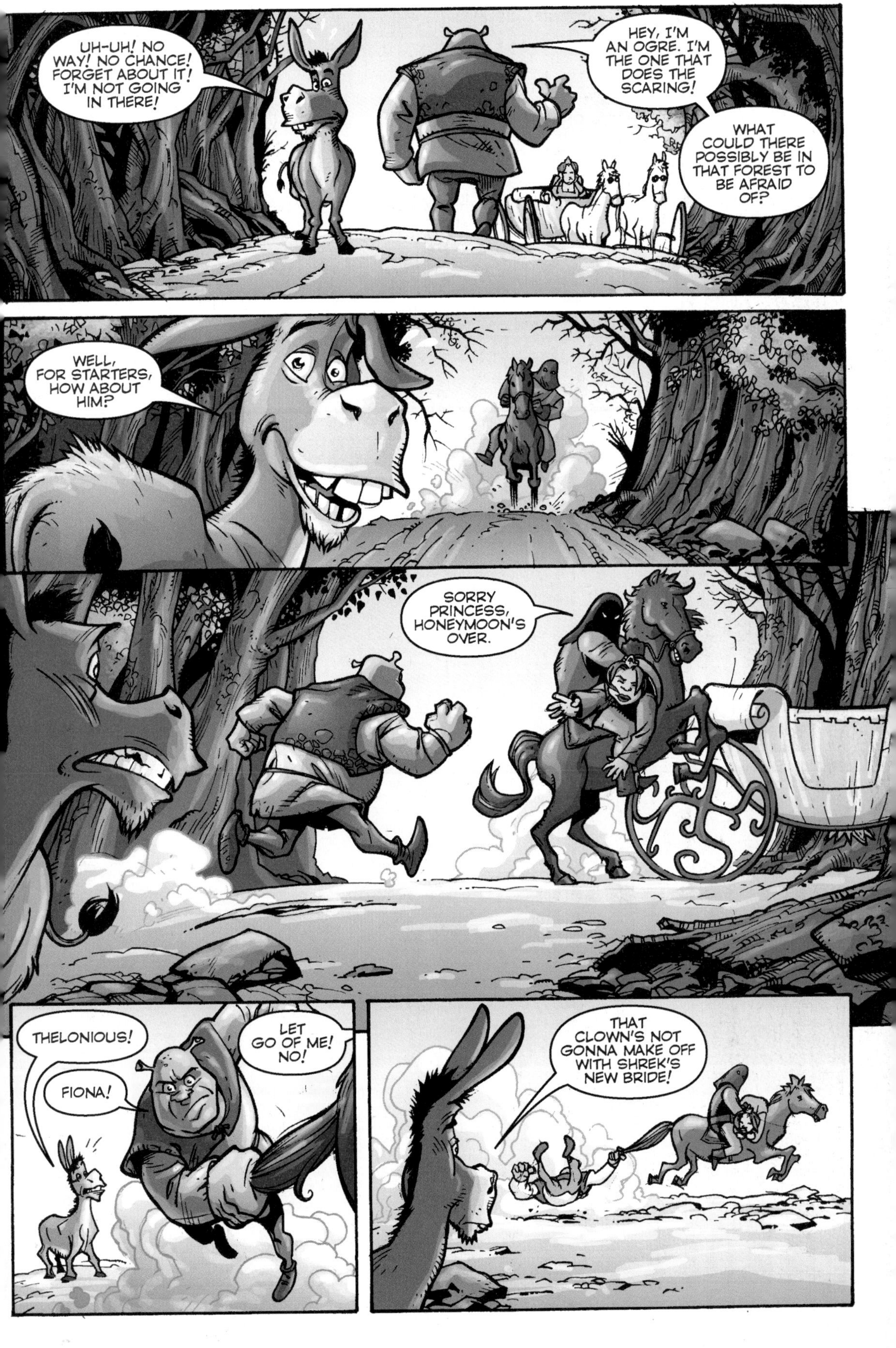
UH-UH! NO WAY! NO CHANCE! FORGET ABOUT IT! I'M NOT GOING IN THERE!
HEY, I'M AN OGRE. I'M THE ONE THAT DOES THE SCARING!
WHAT COULD THERE POSSIBLY BE IN THAT FOREST TO BE AFRAID OF?
WELL, FOR STARTERS, HOW ABOUT HIM?
SORRY PRINCESS, HONEYMOON'S OVER.
THELONIOUS!
FIONA!
LET GO OF ME! NO!
THAT CLOWN'S NOT GONNA MAKE OFF WITH SHREK'S NEW BRIDE!

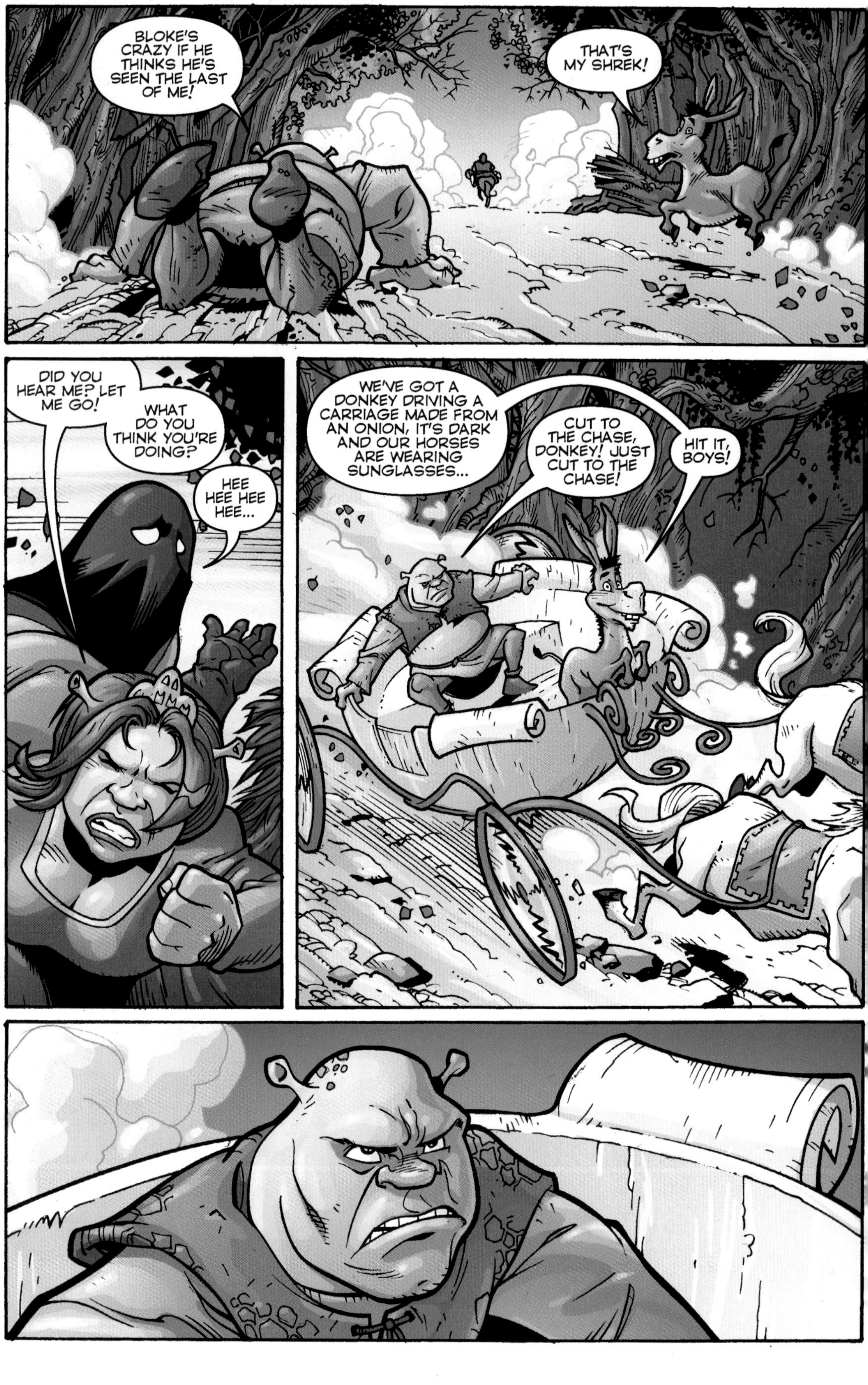
BLOKE'S CRAZY IF HE THINKS HE'S SEEN THE LAST OF ME!
THAT'S MY SHREK!
DID YOU HEAR ME? LET ME GO!
WHAT DO YOU THINK YOU'RE DOING?
HEE HEE HEE HEE...
WE'VE GOT A DONKEY DRIVING A CARRIAGE MADE FROM AN ONION, IT'S DARK AND OUR HORSES ARE WEARING SUNGLASSES...
CUT TO THE CHASE, DONKEY! JUST CUT TO THE CHASE!
HIT IT, BOYS!

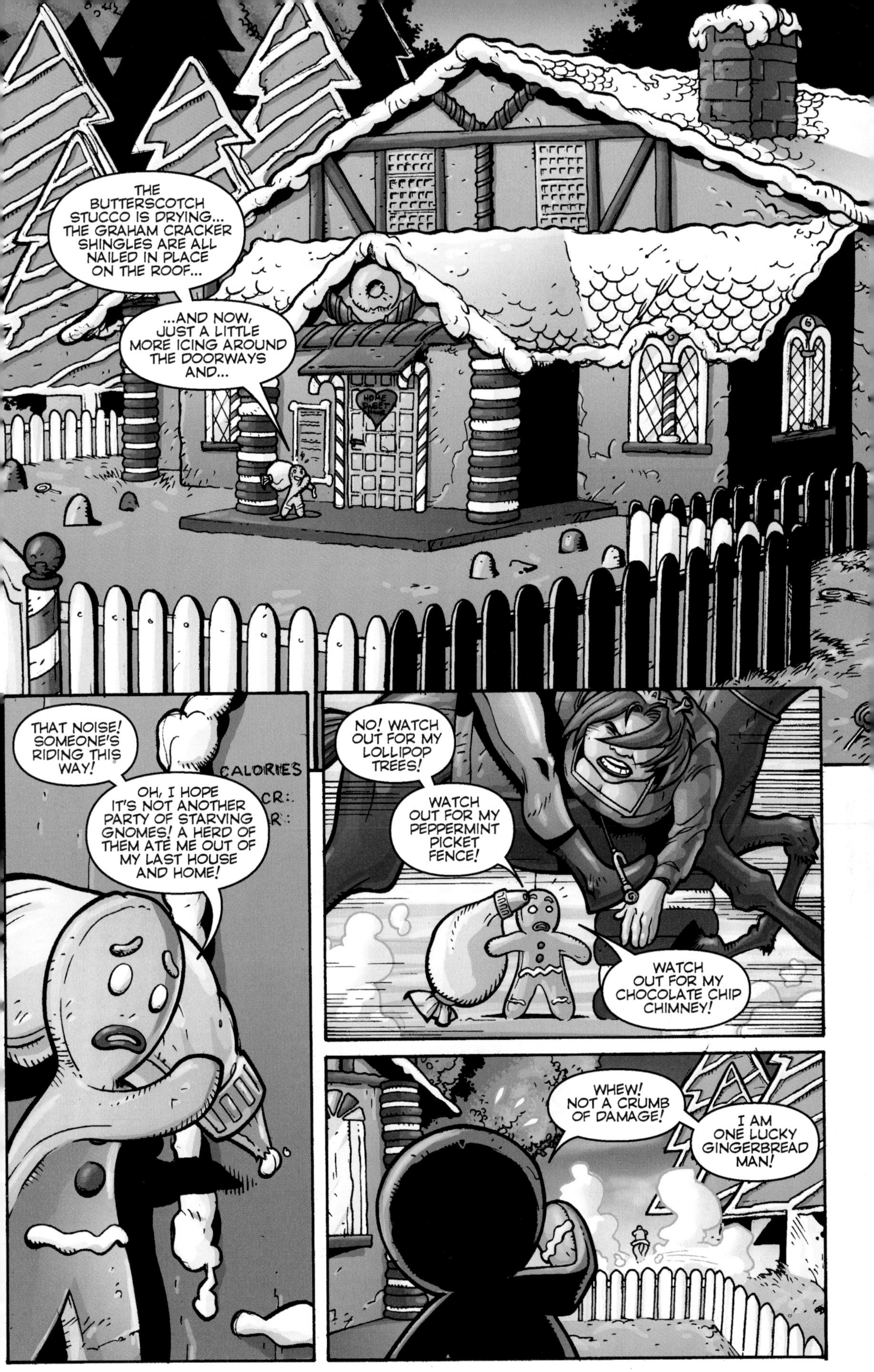
THE BUTTERSCOTCH STUCCO IS DRYING... THE GRAHAM CRACKER SHINGLES ARE ALL NAILED IN PLACE ON THE ROOF...
...AND NOW, JUST A LITTLE MORE ICING AROUND THE DOORWAYS AND...
HOME SWEET HOME
THAT NOISE! SOMEONE'S RIDING THIS WAY!
OH, I HOPE IT'S NOT ANOTHER PARTY OF STARVING GNOMES! A HERD OF THEM ATE ME OUT OF MY LAST HOUSE AND HOME!
CALORIES
NO! WATCH OUT FOR MY LOLLIPOP TREES!
WATCH OUT FOR MY PEPPERMINT PICKET FENCE!
WATCH OUT FOR MY CHOCOLATE CHIP CHIMNEY!
WHEW! NOT A CRUMB OF DAMAGE!
I AM ONE LUCKY GINGERBREAD MAN!

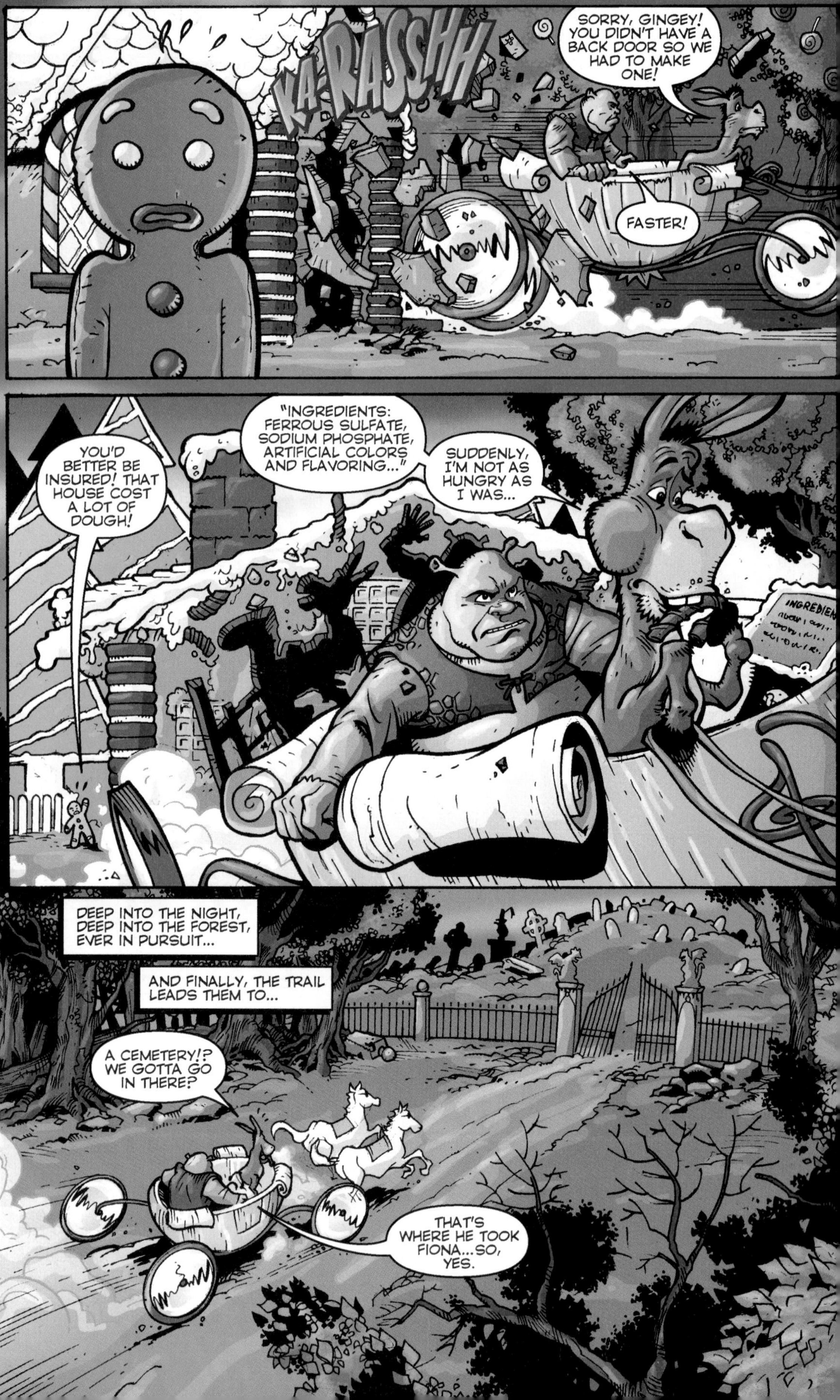
KA-RASSHH
SORRY, GINGEY! YOU DIDN'T HAVE A BACK DOOR SO WE HAD TO MAKE ONE!
FASTER!
YOU'D BETTER BE INSURED! THAT HOUSE COST A LOT OF DOUGH!
"INGREDIENTS: FERROUS SULFATE, SODIUM PHOSPHATE, ARTIFICIAL COLORS AND FLAVORING..."
SUDDENLY, I'M NOT AS HUNGRY AS I WAS...
INGREDIENTS
DEEP INTO THE NIGHT, DEEP INTO THE FOREST, EVER IN PURSUIT...
AND FINALLY, THE TRAIL LEADS THEM TO...
A CEMETERY!? WE GOTTA GO IN THERE?
THAT'S WHERE HE TOOK FIONA...SO, YES.

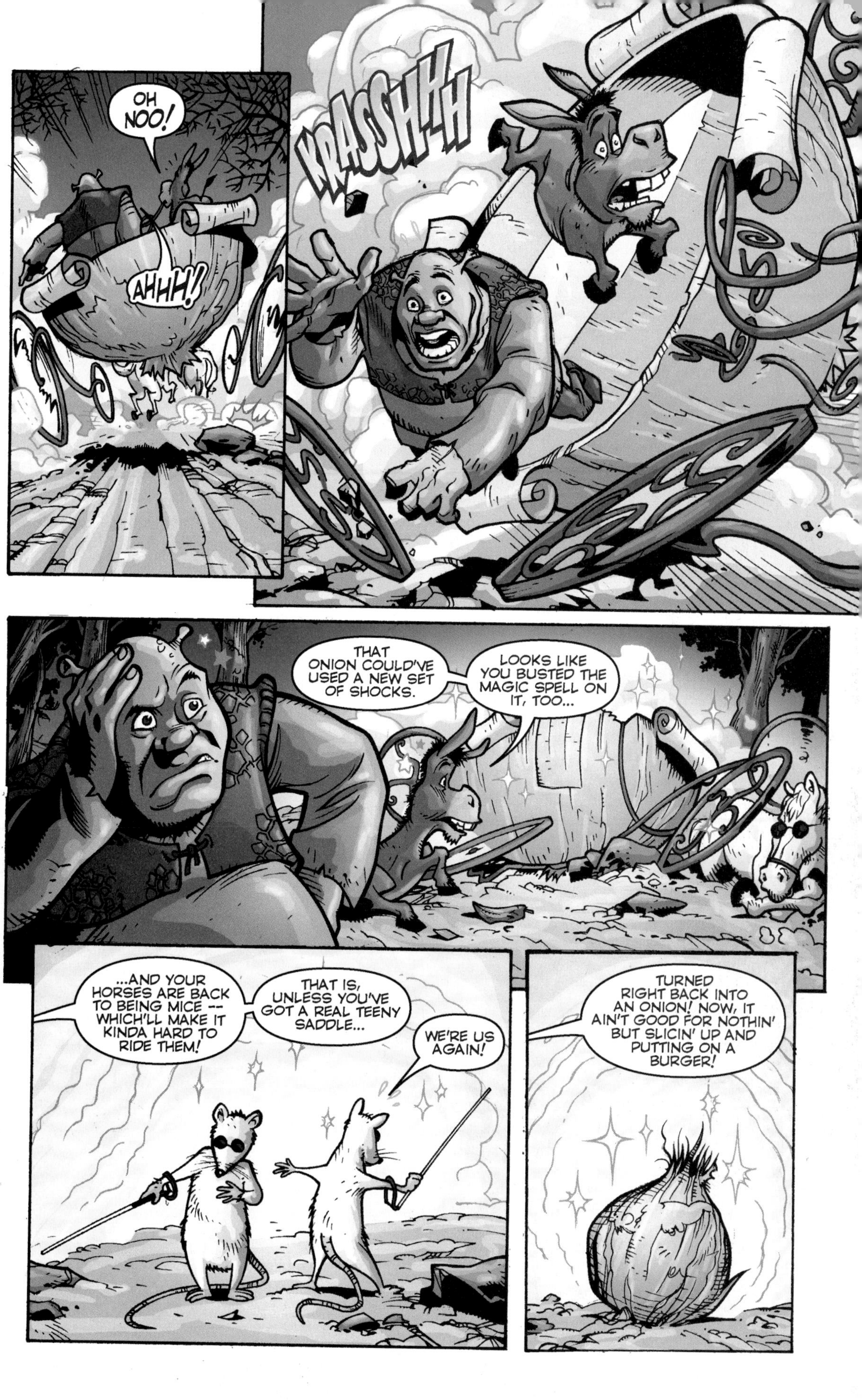

OH NOO!
AHHH!
KRASSHHH
THAT ONION COULD'VE USED A NEW SET OF SHOCKS.
LOOKS LIKE YOU BUSTED THE MAGIC SPELL ON IT, TOO...
...AND YOUR HORSES ARE BACK TO BEING MICE -- WHICH'LL MAKE IT KINDA HARD TO RIDE THEM!
THAT IS, UNLESS YOU'VE GOT A REAL TEENY SADDLE...
WE'RE US AGAIN!
TURNED RIGHT BACK INTO AN ONION! NOW, IT AIN'T GOOD FOR NOTHIN' BUT SLICIN' UP AND PUTTING ON A BURGER!

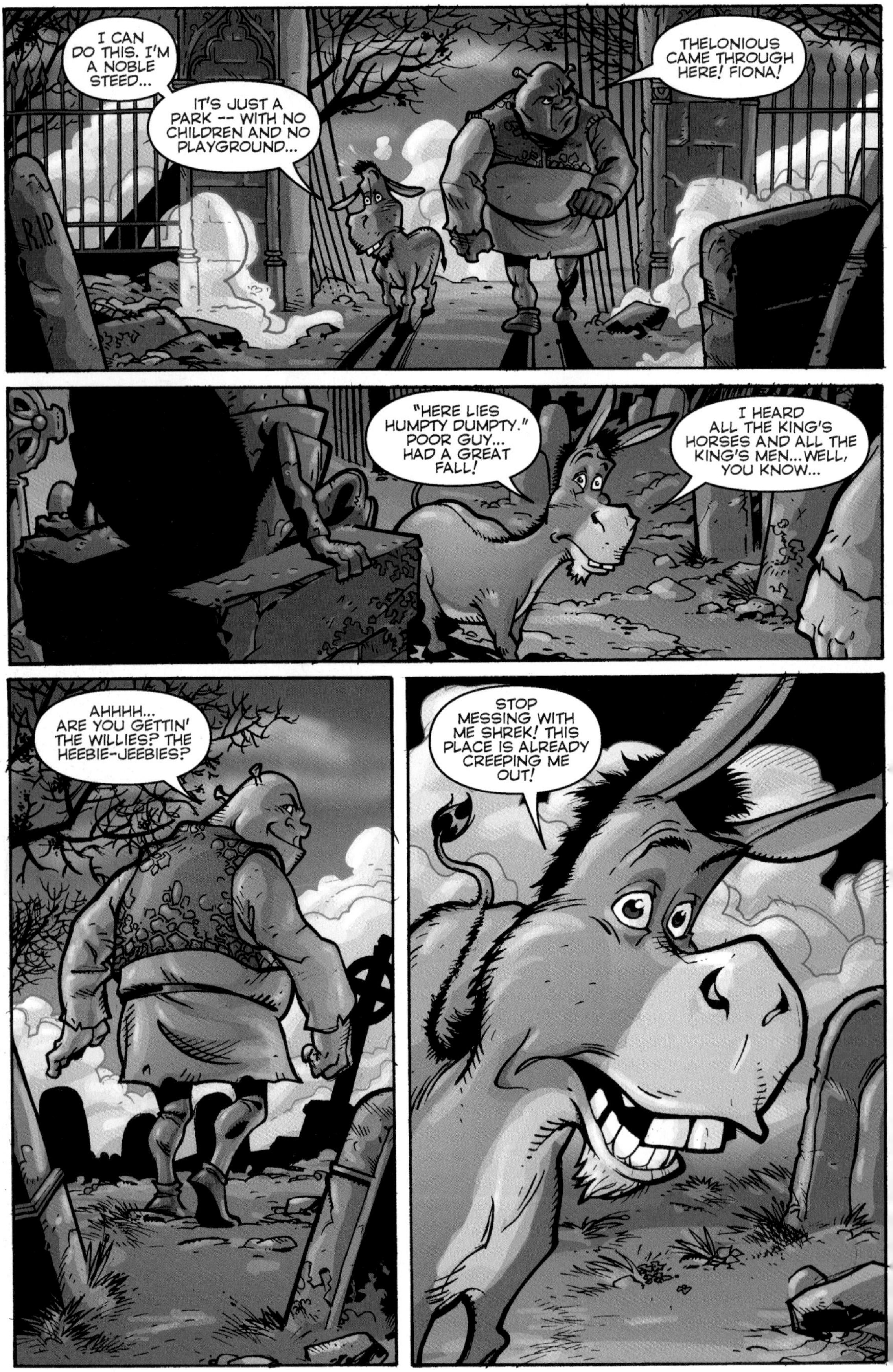
I CAN DO THIS. I'M A NOBLE STEED...
IT'S JUST A PARK -- WITH NO CHILDREN AND NO PLAYGROUND...
THELONIOUS CAME THROUGH HERE! FIONA!
R.I.P.
"HERE LIES HUMPTY DUMPTY." POOR GUY... HAD A GREAT FALL!
I HEARD ALL THE KING'S HORSES AND ALL THE KING'S MEN...WELL, YOU KNOW...
AHHHH... ARE YOU GETTIN' THE WILLIES? THE HEEBIE-JEEBIES?
STOP MESSING WITH ME SHREK! THIS PLACE IS ALREADY CREEPING ME OUT!

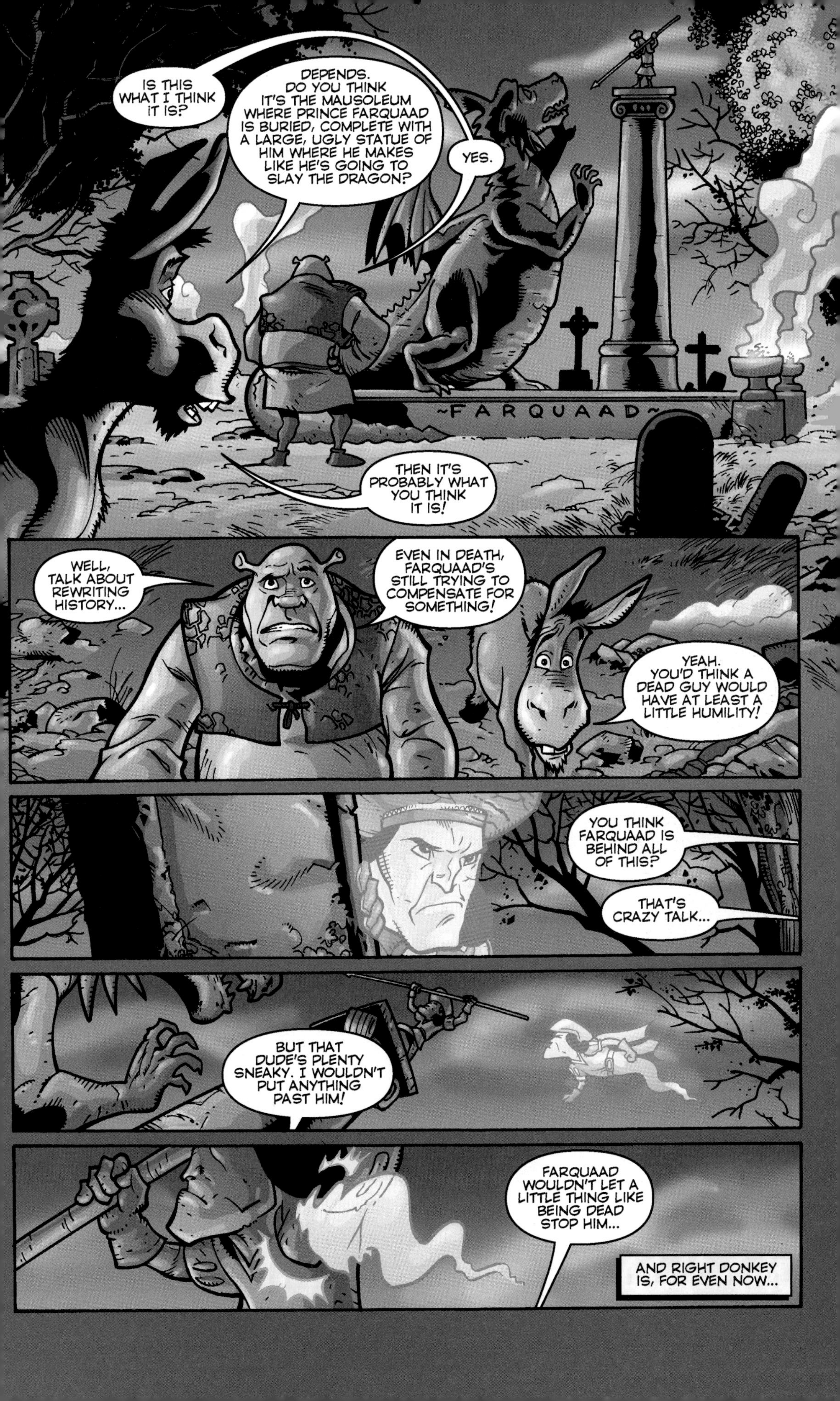
IS THIS WHAT I THINK IT IS?
DEPENDS. DO YOU THINK IT'S THE MAUSOLEUM WHERE PRINCE FARQUAAD IS BURIED, COMPLETE WITH A LARGE, UGLY STATUE OF HIM WHERE HE MAKES LIKE HE'S GOING TO SLAY THE DRAGON?
YES.
~FARQUAAD~
THEN IT'S PROBABLY WHAT YOU THINK IT IS!
WELL, TALK ABOUT REWRITING HISTORY...
EVEN IN DEATH, FARQUAAD'S STILL TRYING TO COMPENSATE FOR SOMETHING!
YEAH. YOU'D THINK A DEAD GUY WOULD HAVE AT LEAST A LITTLE HUMILITY!
YOU THINK FARQUAAD IS BEHIND ALL OF THIS?
THAT'S CRAZY TALK...
BUT THAT DUDE'S PLENTY SNEAKY. I WOULDN'T PUT ANYTHING PAST HIM!
FARQUAAD WOULDN'T LET A LITTLE THING LIKE BEING DEAD STOP HIM...
AND RIGHT DONKEY IS, FOR EVEN NOW...

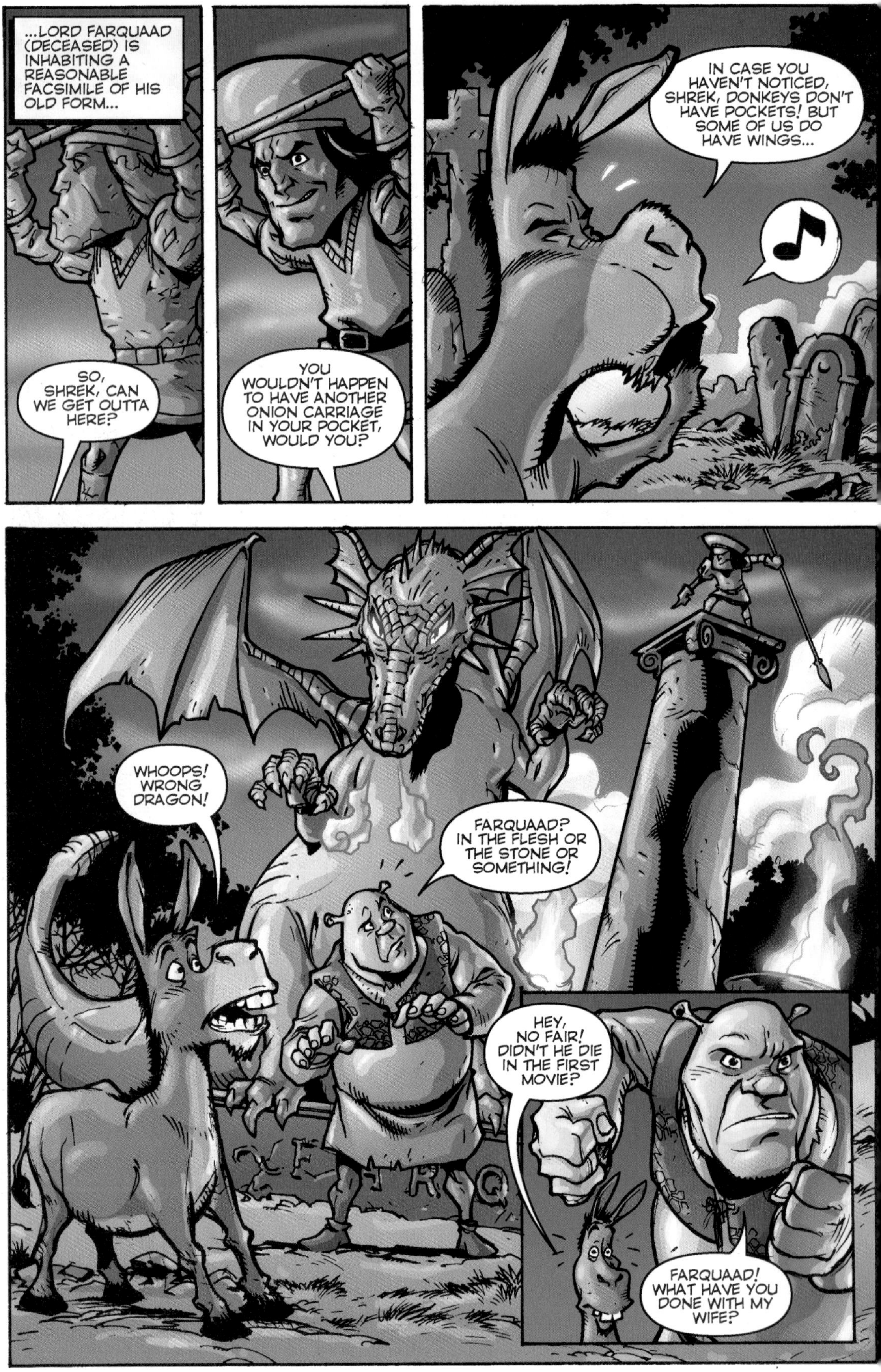
...LORD FARQUAAD (DECEASED) IS INHABITING A REASONABLE FACSIMILE OF HIS OLD FORM...
SO, SHREK, CAN WE GET OUTTA HERE?
YOU WOULDN'T HAPPEN TO HAVE ANOTHER ONION CARRIAGE IN YOUR POCKET, WOULD YOU?
IN CASE YOU HAVEN'T NOTICED, SHREK, DONKEYS DON'T HAVE POCKETS! BUT SOME OF US DO HAVE WINGS...
♪
WHOOPS! WRONG DRAGON!
FARQUAAD? IN THE FLESH OR THE STONE OR SOMETHING!
HEY, NO FAIR! DIDN'T HE DIE IN THE FIRST MOVIE?
FARQUAAD! WHAT HAVE YOU DONE WITH MY WIFE?

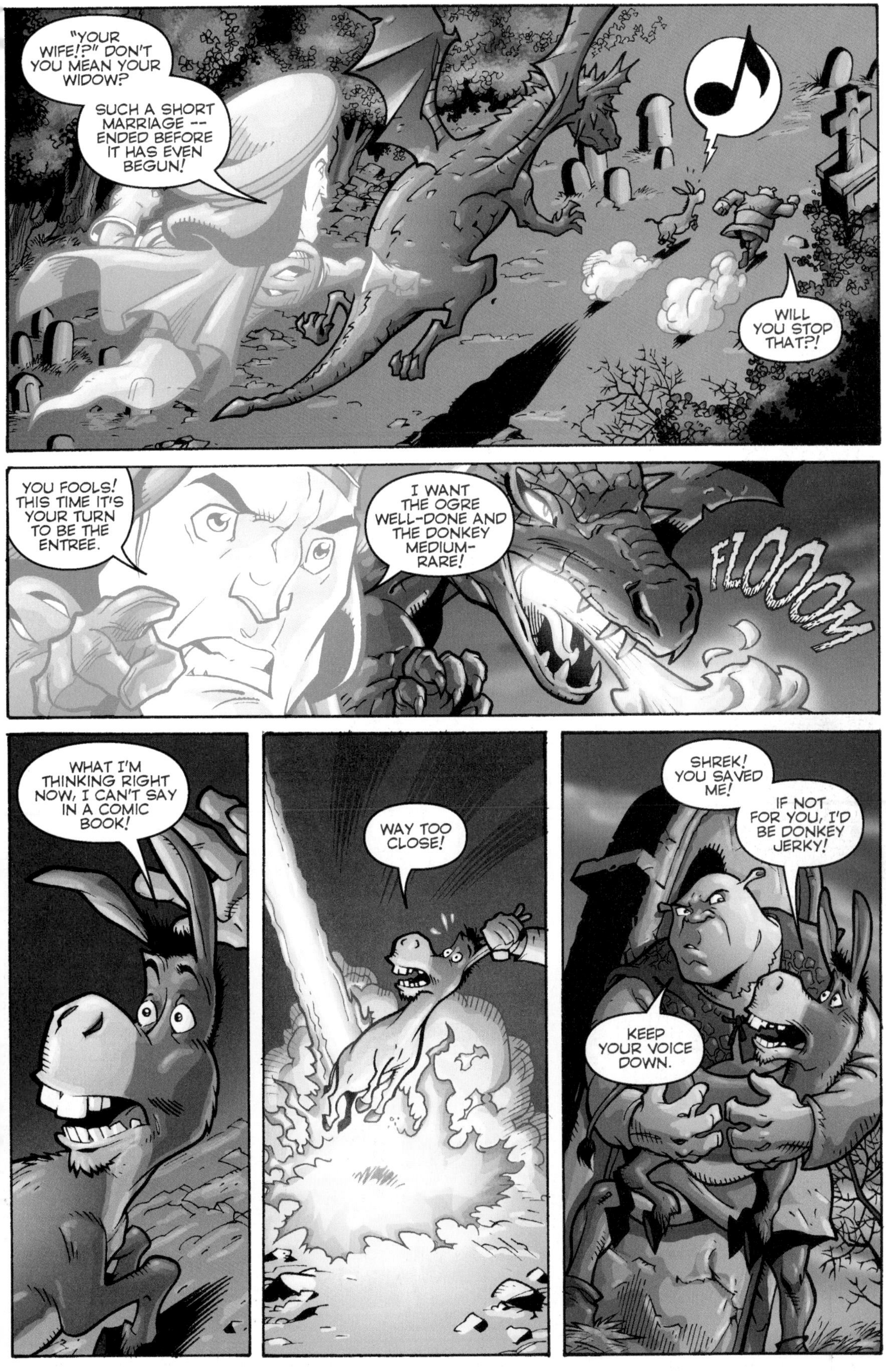
"YOUR WIFE!?" DON'T YOU MEAN YOUR WIDOW?
SUCH A SHORT MARRIAGE -- ENDED BEFORE IT HAS EVEN BEGUN!
WILL YOU STOP THAT?!
YOU FOOLS! THIS TIME IT'S YOUR TURN TO BE THE ENTREE.
I WANT THE OGRE WELL-DONE AND THE DONKEY MEDIUM-RARE!
FLOOOM
WHAT I'M THINKING RIGHT NOW, I CAN'T SAY IN A COMIC BOOK!
WAY TOO CLOSE!
SHREK! YOU SAVED ME!
IF NOT FOR YOU, I'D BE DONKEY JERKY!
KEEP YOUR VOICE DOWN.

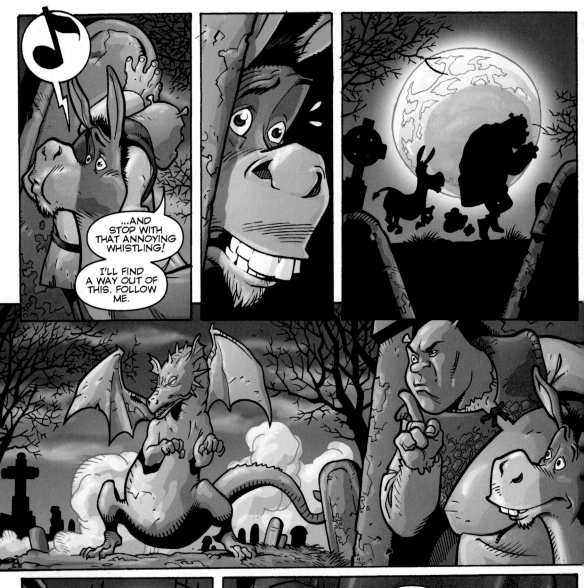

...AND STOP WITH THAT ANNOYING WHISTLING!

I'LL FIND A WAY OUT OF THIS. FOLLOW ME.

UH-OH.

YOU GO FIRST. I'LL BE DESSERT!

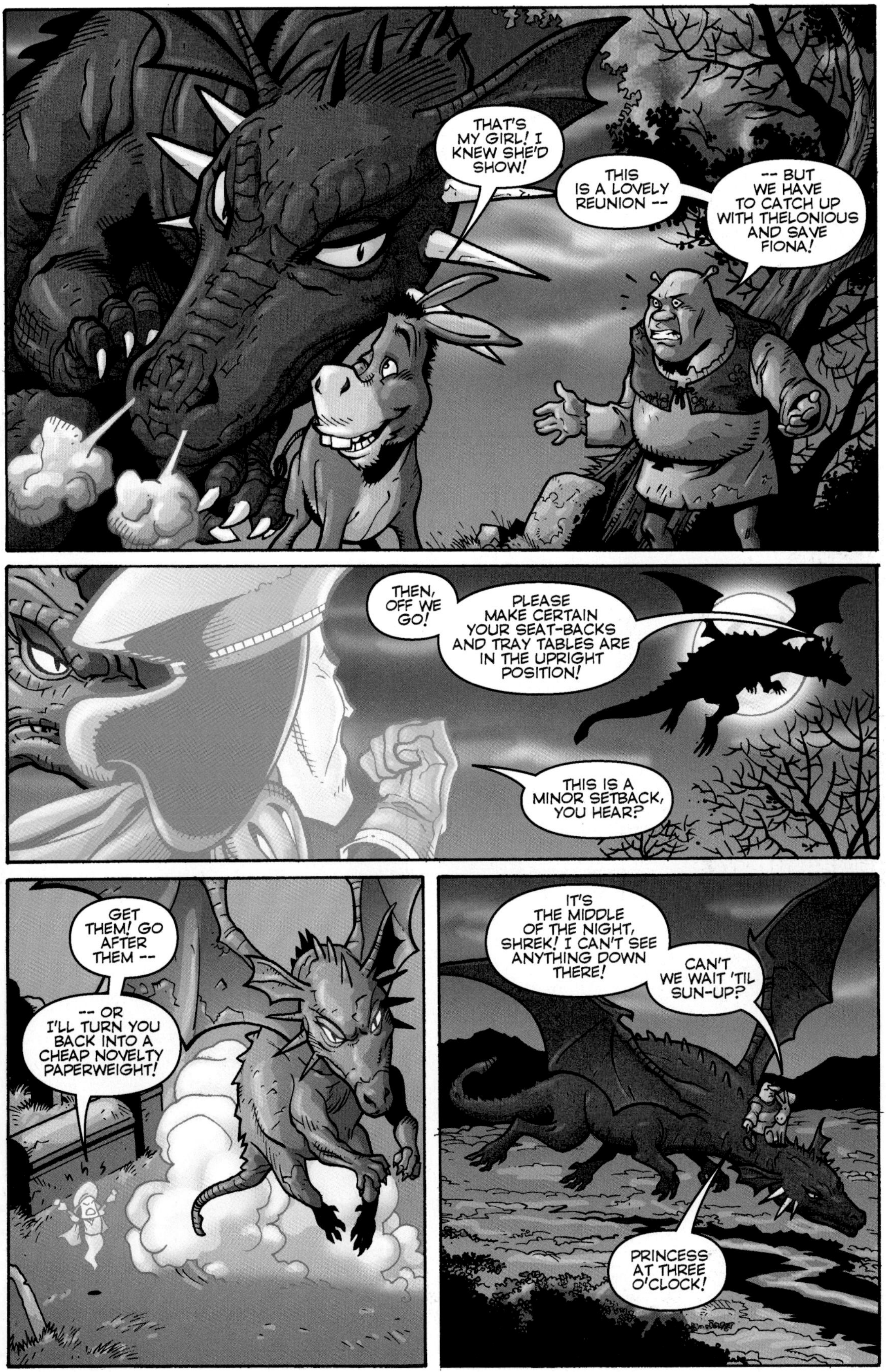
THAT'S MY GIRL! I KNEW SHE'D SHOW!
THIS IS A LOVELY REUNION --
-- BUT WE HAVE TO CATCH UP WITH THELONIOUS AND SAVE FIONA!
THEN, OFF WE GO!
PLEASE MAKE CERTAIN YOUR SEAT-BACKS AND TRAY TABLES ARE IN THE UPRIGHT POSITION!
THIS IS A MINOR SETBACK, YOU HEAR?
GET THEM! GO AFTER THEM --
-- OR I'LL TURN YOU BACK INTO A CHEAP NOVELTY PAPERWEIGHT!
IT'S THE MIDDLE OF THE NIGHT, SHREK! I CAN'T SEE ANYTHING DOWN THERE!
CAN'T WE WAIT 'TIL SUN-UP?
PRINCESS AT THREE O'CLOCK!

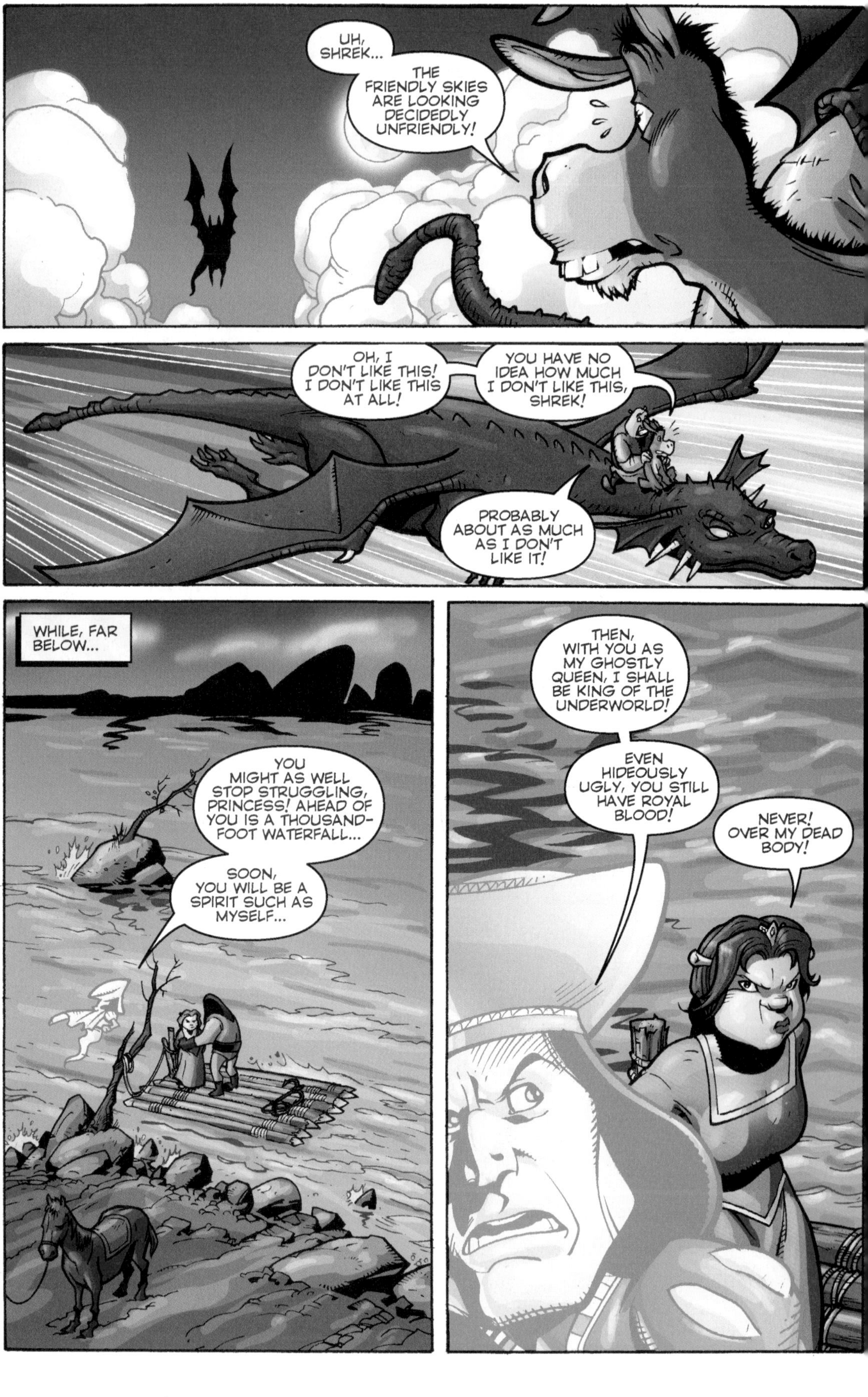
UH, SHREK...
THE FRIENDLY SKIES ARE LOOKING DECIDEDLY UNFRIENDLY!
OH, I DON'T LIKE THIS! I DON'T LIKE THIS AT ALL!
YOU HAVE NO IDEA HOW MUCH I DON'T LIKE THIS, SHREK!
PROBABLY ABOUT AS MUCH AS I DON'T LIKE IT!
WHILE, FAR BELOW...
YOU MIGHT AS WELL STOP STRUGGLING, PRINCESS! AHEAD OF YOU IS A THOUSAND-FOOT WATERFALL...
SOON, YOU WILL BE A SPIRIT SUCH AS MYSELF...
THEN, WITH YOU AS MY GHOSTLY QUEEN, I SHALL BE KING OF THE UNDERWORLD!
EVEN HIDEOUSLY UGLY, YOU STILL HAVE ROYAL BLOOD!
NEVER! OVER MY DEAD BODY!

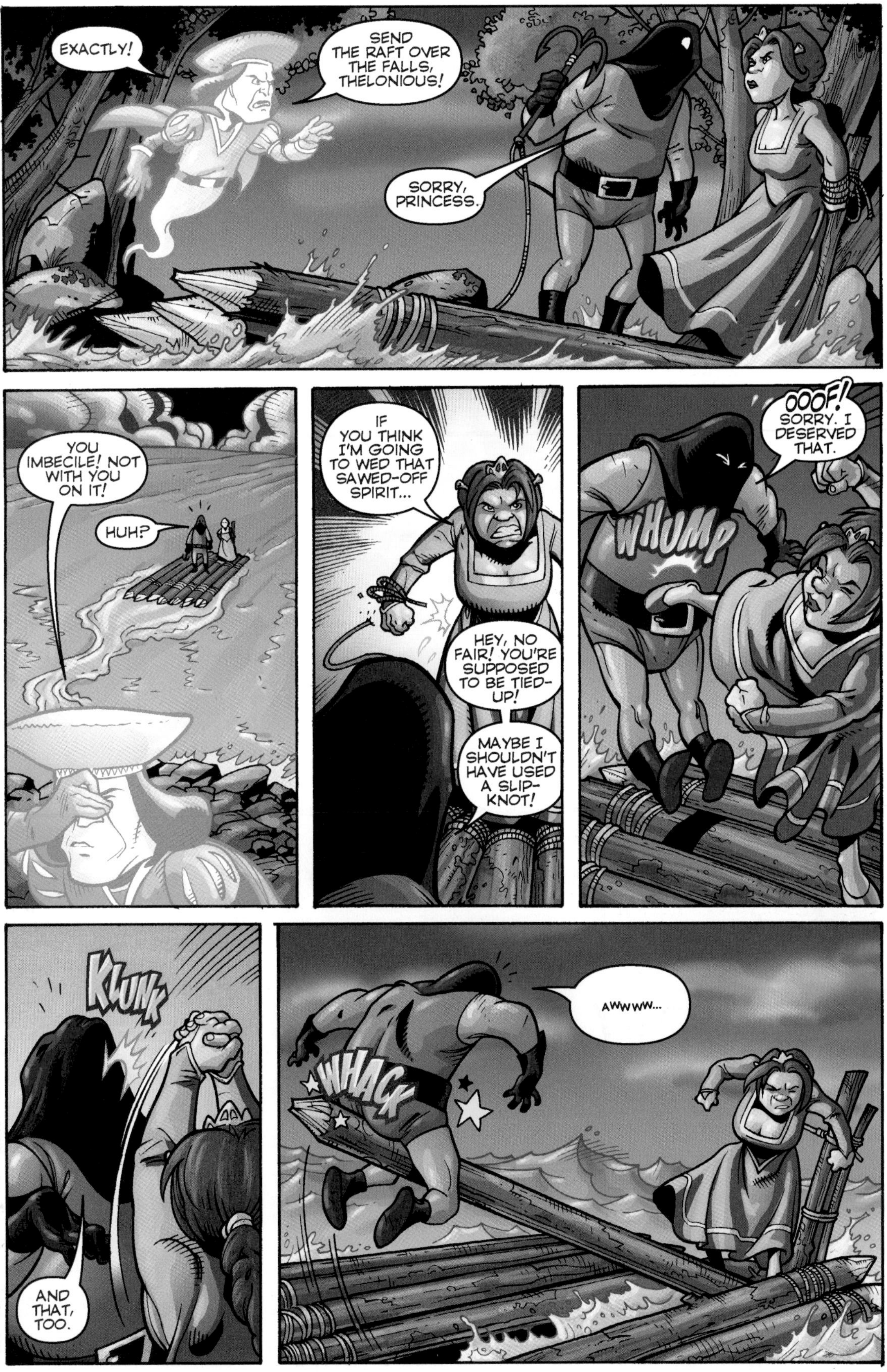

EXACTLY!
SEND THE RAFT OVER THE FALLS, THELONIOUS!
SORRY, PRINCESS.
YOU IMBECILE! NOT WITH YOU ON IT!
HUH?
IF YOU THINK I'M GOING TO WED THAT SAWED-OFF SPIRIT...
HEY, NO FAIR! YOU'RE SUPPOSED TO BE TIED-UP!
MAYBE I SHOULDN'T HAVE USED A SLIP-KNOT!
OOOF!
SORRY. I DESERVED THAT.
WHUMP
KLUNK
AND THAT, TOO.
AWWWW...
WHACK

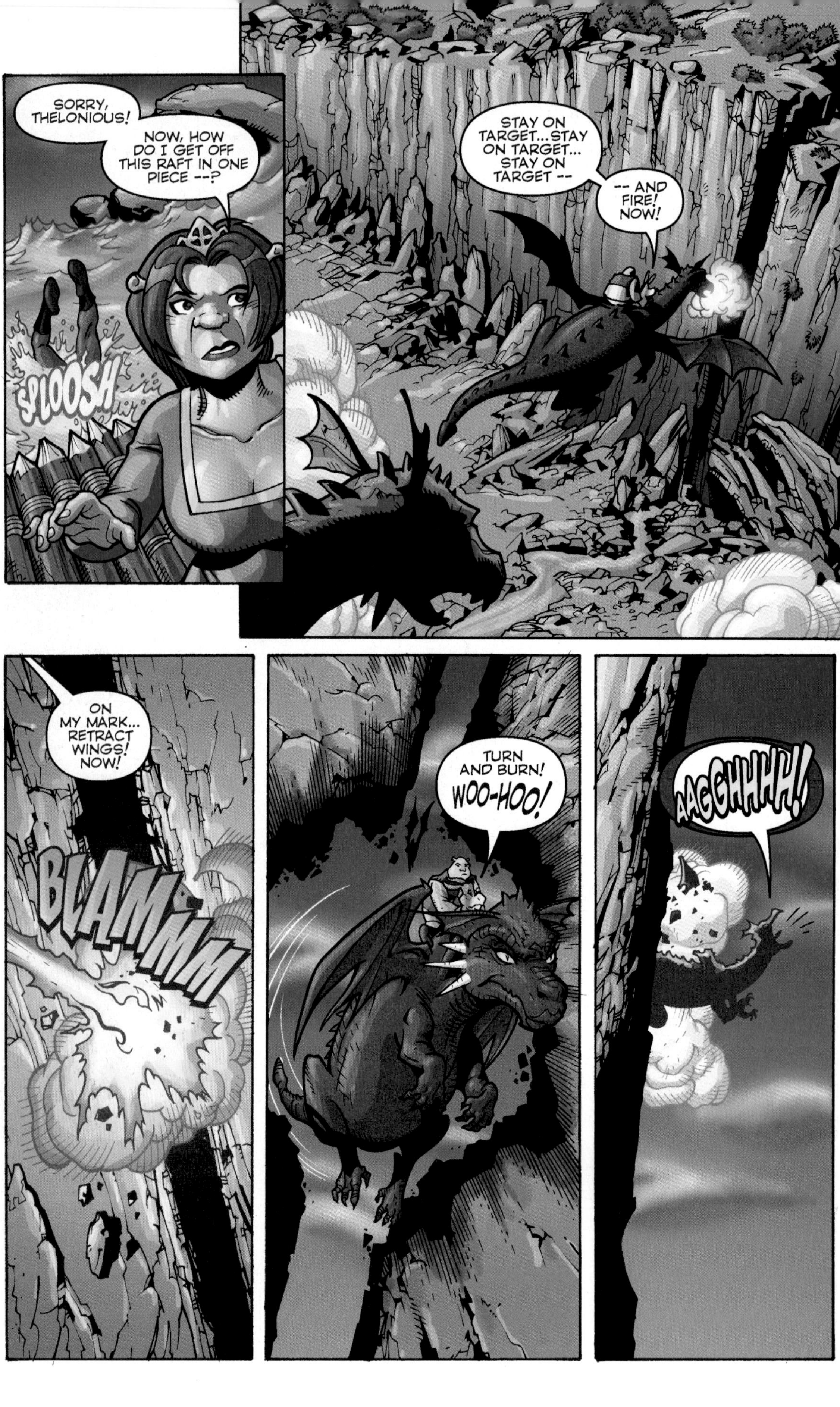
SORRY, THELONIOUS!
NOW, HOW DO I GET OFF THIS RAFT IN ONE PIECE --?
SPLOOSH
STAY ON TARGET...STAY ON TARGET... STAY ON TARGET --
-- AND FIRE! NOW!
ON MY MARK... RETRACT WINGS! NOW!
BLAMMM
TURN AND BURN! WOO-HOO!
AAGHHHH!

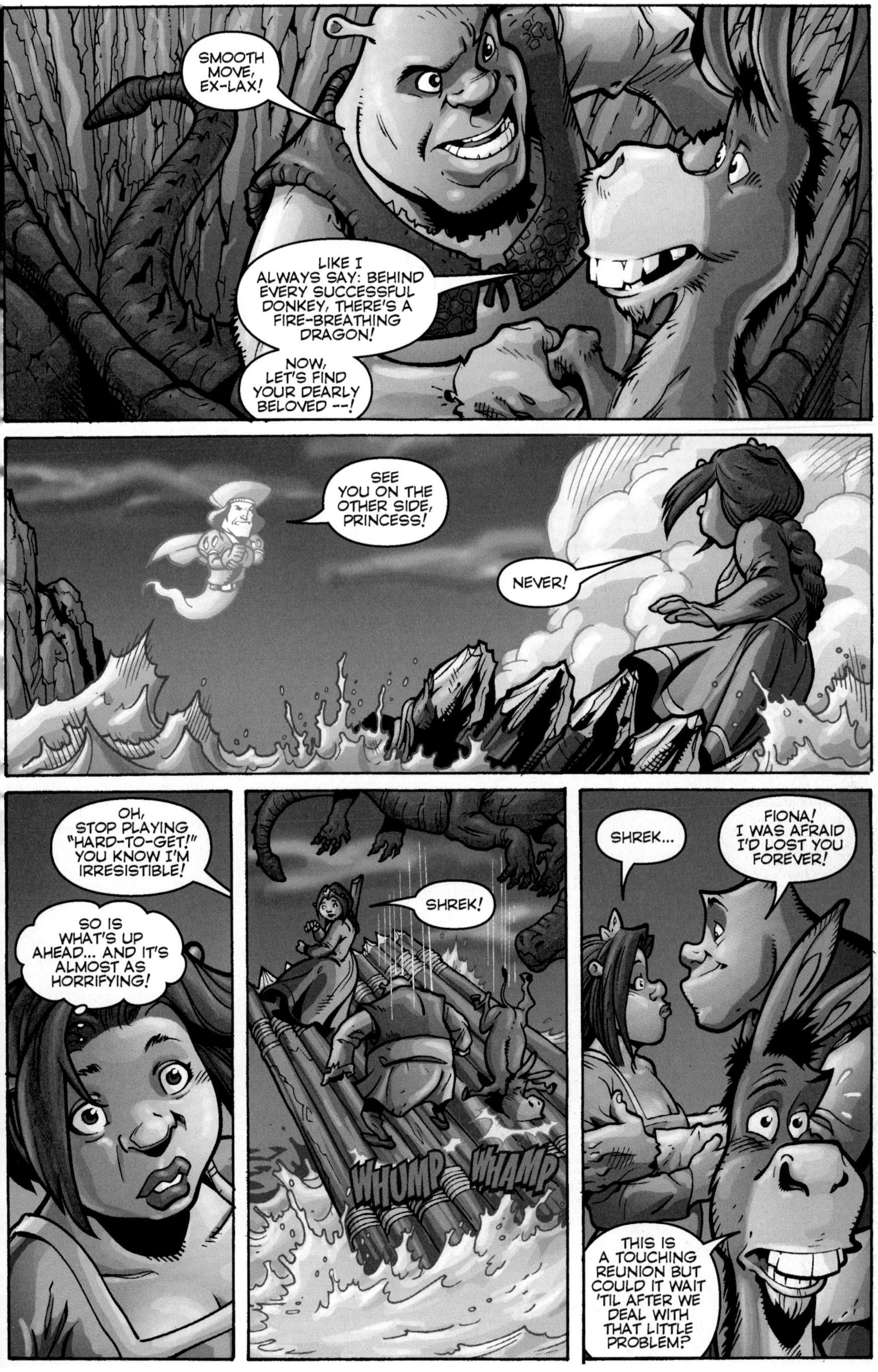

SMOOTH MOVE, EX-LAX!
LIKE I ALWAYS SAY: BEHIND EVERY SUCCESSFUL DONKEY, THERE'S A FIRE-BREATHING DRAGON!
NOW, LET'S FIND YOUR DEARLY BELOVED --!
SEE YOU ON THE OTHER SIDE, PRINCESS!
NEVER!
OH, STOP PLAYING "HARD-TO-GET!" YOU KNOW I'M IRRESISTIBLE!
SO IS WHAT'S UP AHEAD... AND IT'S ALMOST AS HORRIFYING!
SHREK!
WHUMP
WHAMP
SHREK...
FIONA! I WAS AFRAID I'D LOST YOU FOREVER!
THIS IS A TOUCHING REUNION BUT COULD IT WAIT 'TIL AFTER WE DEAL WITH THAT LITTLE PROBLEM?

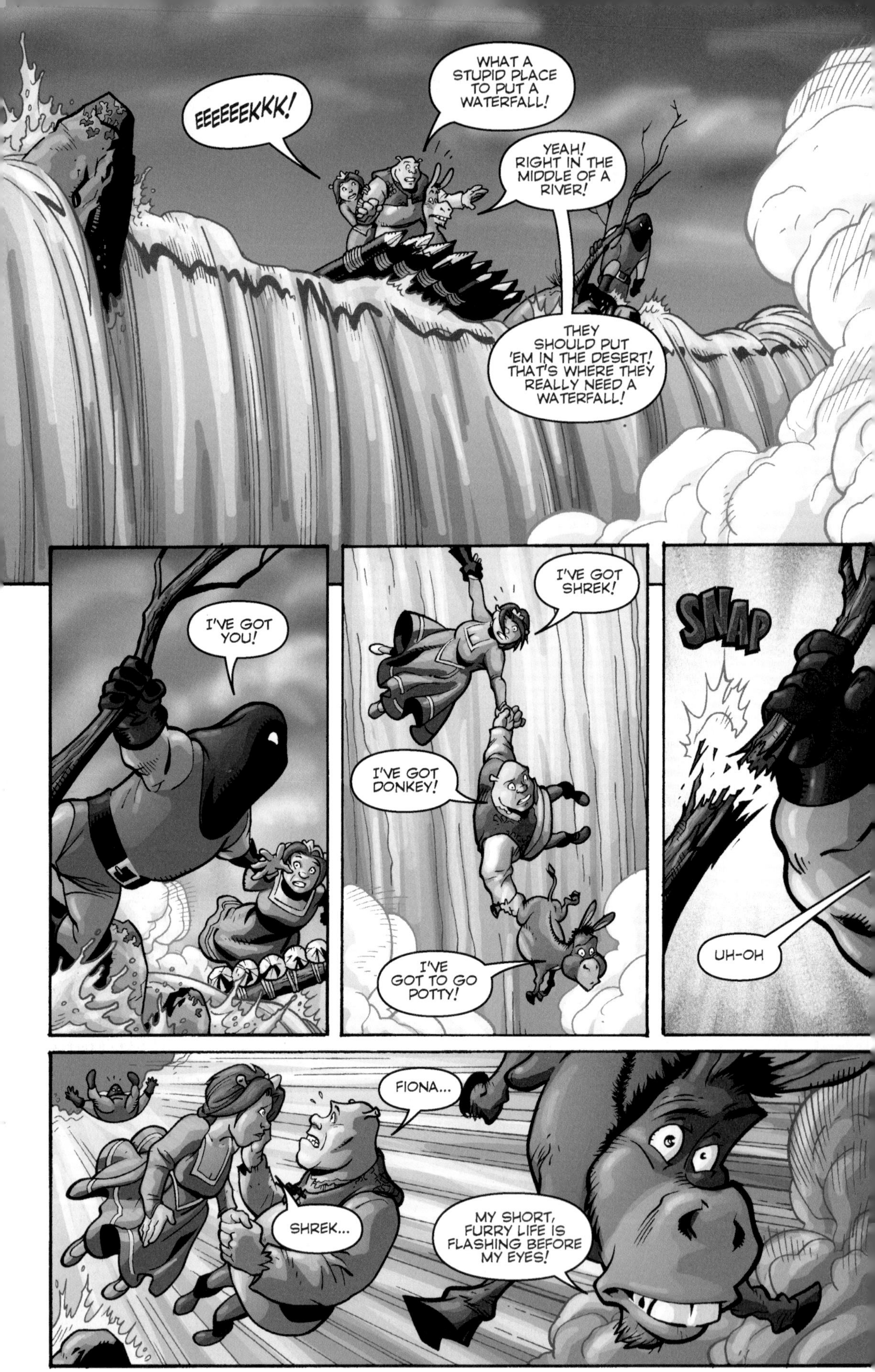
EEEEEEKKK!
WHAT A STUPID PLACE TO PUT A WATERFALL!
YEAH! RIGHT IN THE MIDDLE OF A RIVER!
THEY SHOULD PUT 'EM IN THE DESERT! THAT'S WHERE THEY REALLY NEED A WATERFALL!
I'VE GOT YOU!
I'VE GOT SHREK!
I'VE GOT DONKEY!
I'VE GOT TO GO POTTY!
SNAP
UH-OH
FIONA...
SHREK...
MY SHORT, FURRY LIFE IS FLASHING BEFORE MY EYES!

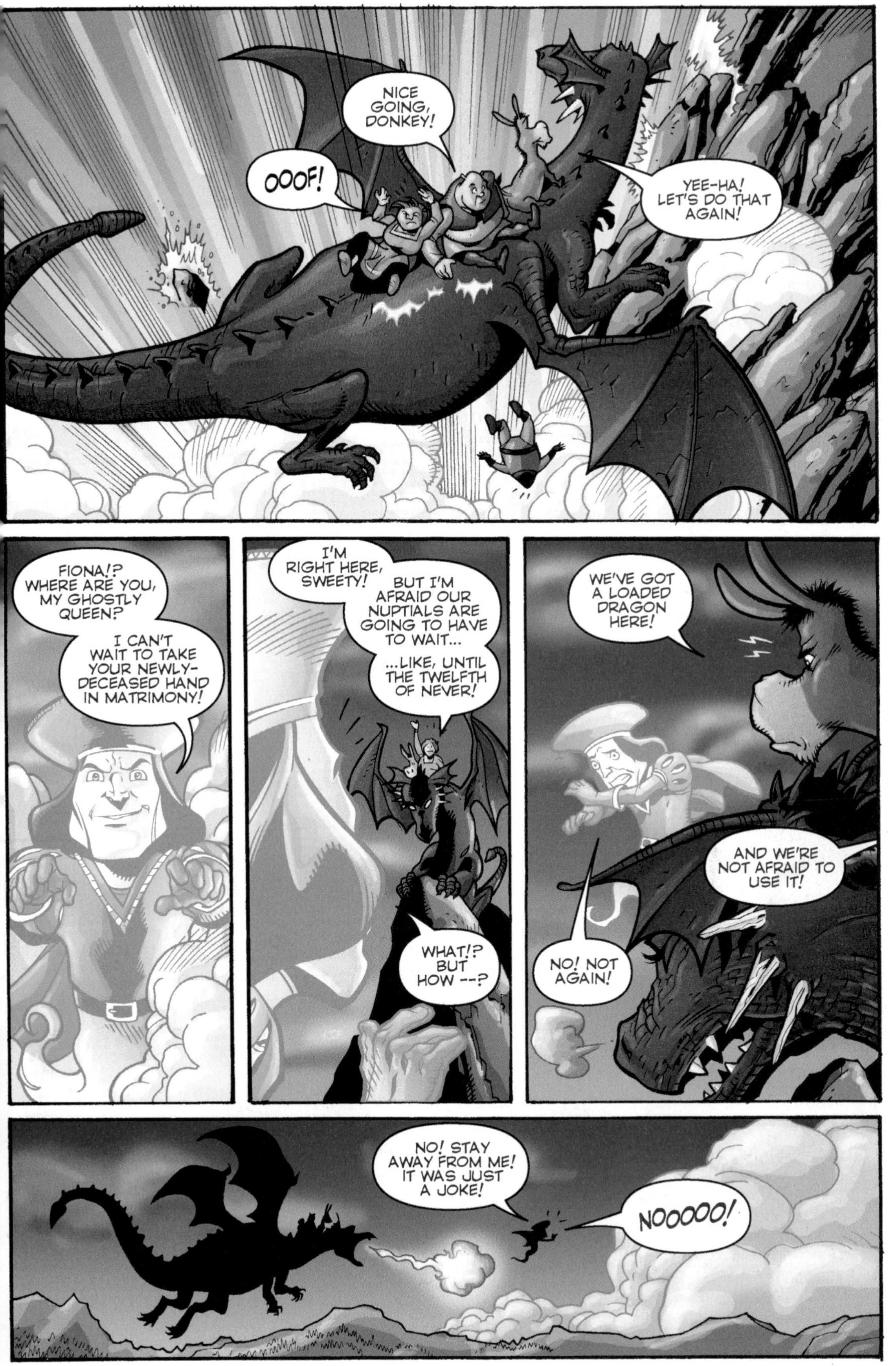
NICE GOING, DONKEY!
OOOF!
YEE-HA! LET'S DO THAT AGAIN!
FIONA!? WHERE ARE YOU, MY GHOSTLY QUEEN?
I CAN'T WAIT TO TAKE YOUR NEWLY-DECEASED HAND IN MATRIMONY!
I'M RIGHT HERE, SWEETY!
BUT I'M AFRAID OUR NUPTIALS ARE GOING TO HAVE TO WAIT...
...LIKE, UNTIL THE TWELFTH OF NEVER!
WHAT!? BUT HOW --?
WE'VE GOT A LOADED DRAGON HERE!
AND WE'RE NOT AFRAID TO USE IT!
NO! NOT AGAIN!
NO! STAY AWAY FROM ME! IT WAS JUST A JOKE!
NOOOOO!

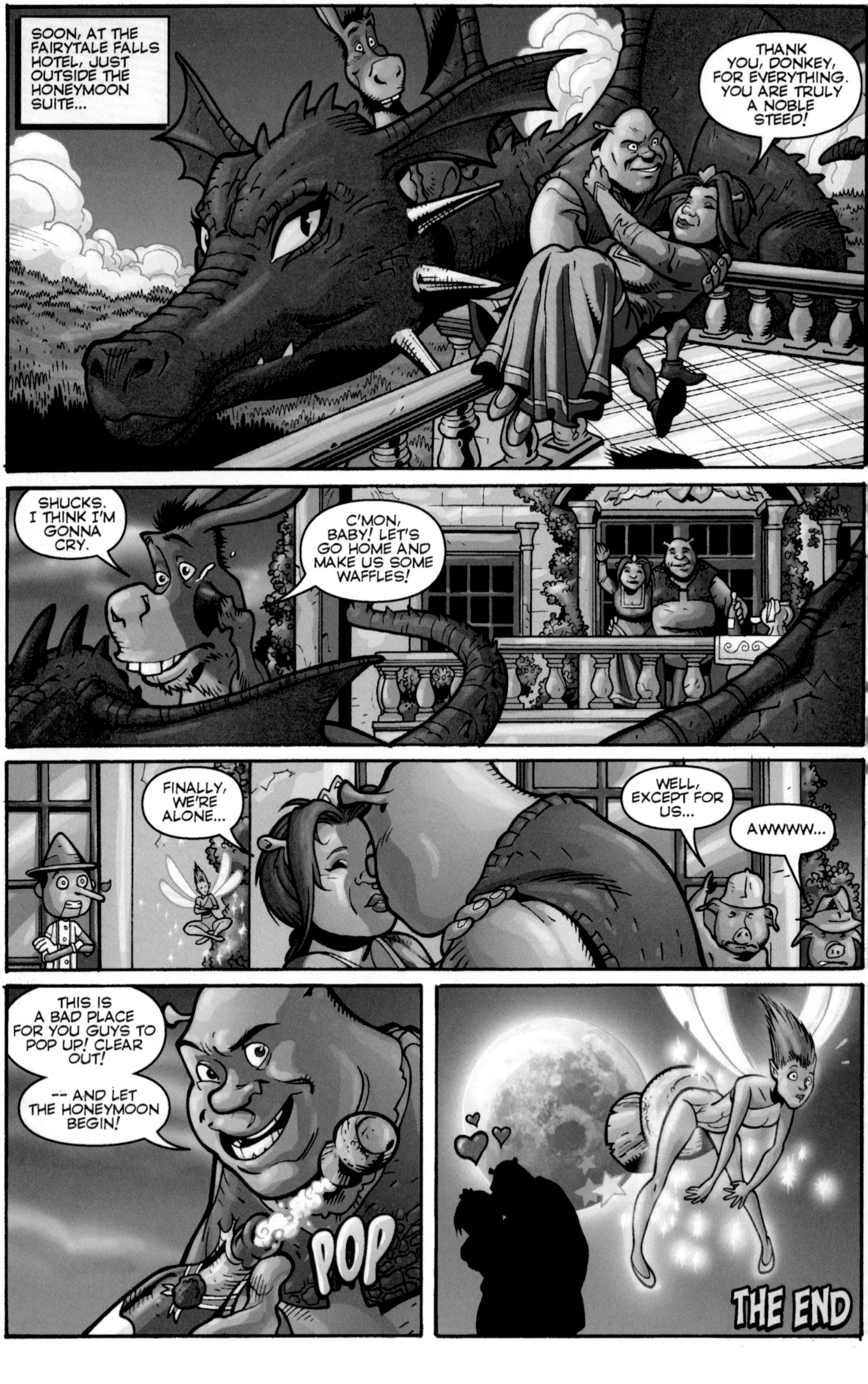
SOON, AT THE FAIRYTALE FALLS HOTEL, JUST OUTSIDE THE HONEYMOON SUITE...
THANK YOU, DONKEY, FOR EVERYTHING. YOU ARE TRULY A NOBLE STEED!
SHUCKS. I THINK I'M GONNA CRY.
C'MON, BABY! LET'S GO HOME AND MAKE US SOME WAFFLES!
FINALLY, WE'RE ALONE...
WELL, EXCEPT FOR US...
AWWWW...
THIS IS A BAD PLACE FOR YOU GUYS TO POP UP! CLEAR OUT!
-- AND LET THE HONEYMOON BEGIN!
POP
THE END

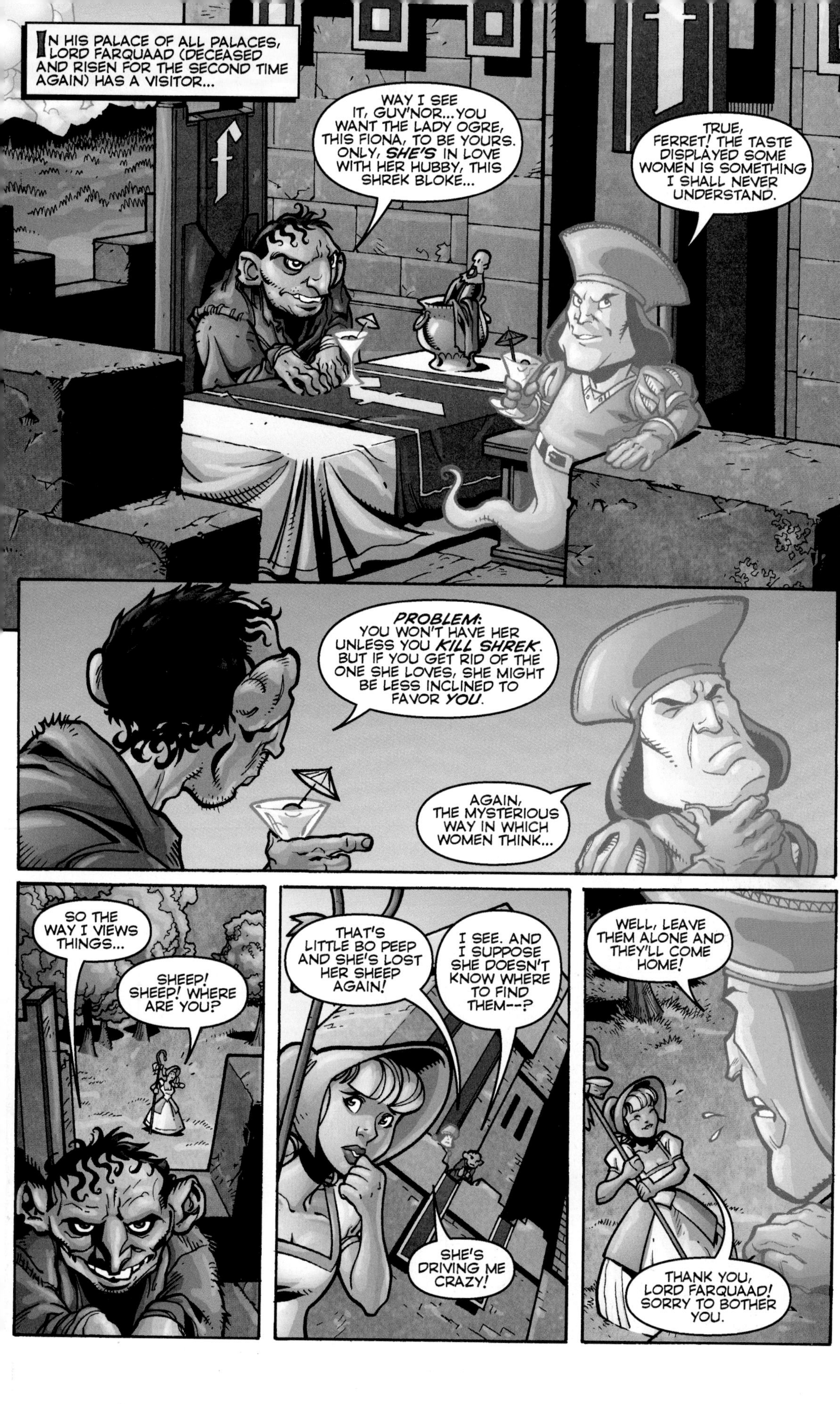
IN HIS PALACE OF ALL PALACES, LORD FARQUAAD (DECEASED AND RISEN FOR THE SECOND TIME AGAIN) HAS A VISITOR...
WAY I SEE IT, GUV'NOR... YOU WANT THE LADY OGRE, THIS FIONA, TO BE YOURS. ONLY, SHE'S IN LOVE WITH HER HUBBY, THIS SHREK BLOKE...
TRUE, FERRET! THE TASTE DISPLAYED SOME WOMEN IS SOMETHING I SHALL NEVER UNDERSTAND.
PROBLEM: YOU WON'T HAVE HER UNLESS YOU KILL SHREK. BUT IF YOU GET RID OF THE ONE SHE LOVES, SHE MIGHT BE LESS INCLINED TO FAVOR YOU.
AGAIN, THE MYSTERIOUS WAY IN WHICH WOMEN THINK...
SO THE WAY I VIEWS THINGS...
SHEEP! SHEEP! WHERE ARE YOU?
THAT'S LITTLE BO PEEP AND SHE'S LOST HER SHEEP AGAIN!
I SEE. AND I SUPPOSE SHE DOESN'T KNOW WHERE TO FIND THEM--?
SHE'S DRIVING ME CRAZY!
WELL, LEAVE THEM ALONE AND THEY'LL COME HOME!
THANK YOU, LORD FARQUAAD! SORRY TO BOTHER YOU.

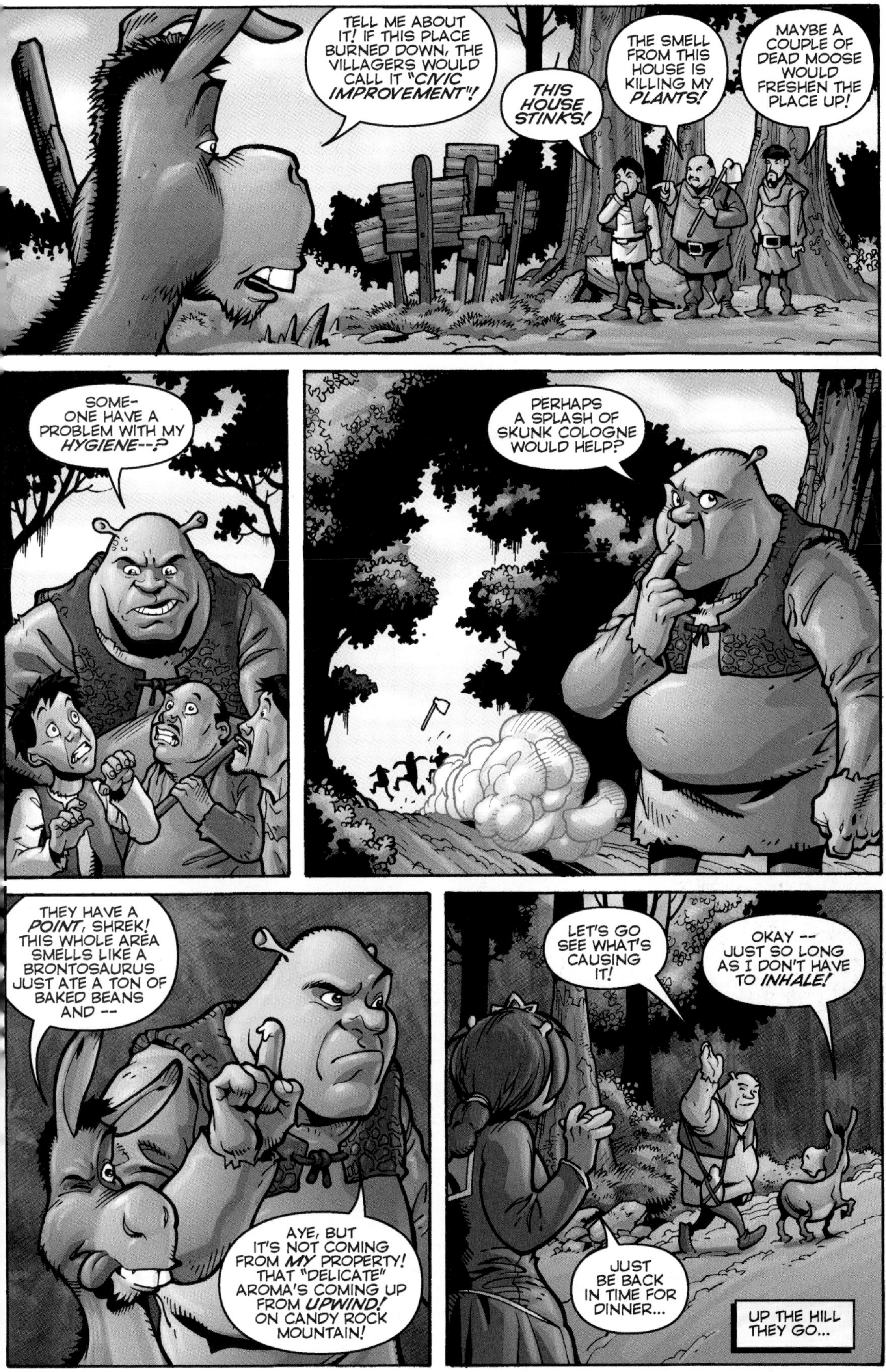

TELL ME ABOUT IT! IF THIS PLACE BURNED DOWN, THE VILLAGERS WOULD CALL IT "CIVIC IMPROVEMENT"!
THIS HOUSE STINKS!
THE SMELL FROM THIS HOUSE IS KILLING MY PLANTS!
MAYBE A COUPLE OF DEAD MOOSE WOULD FRESHEN THE PLACE UP!
SOME-ONE HAVE A PROBLEM WITH MY HYGIENE--?
PERHAPS A SPLASH OF SKUNK COLOGNE WOULD HELP?
THEY HAVE A POINT, SHREK! THIS WHOLE AREA SMELLS LIKE A BRONTOSAURUS JUST ATE A TON OF BAKED BEANS AND --
AYE, BUT IT'S NOT COMING FROM MY PROPERTY! THAT "DELICATE" AROMA'S COMING UP FROM UPWIND! ON CANDY ROCK MOUNTAIN!
LET'S GO SEE WHAT'S CAUSING IT!
OKAY -- JUST SO LONG AS I DON'T HAVE TO INHALE!
JUST BE BACK IN TIME FOR DINNER...
UP THE HILL THEY GO...

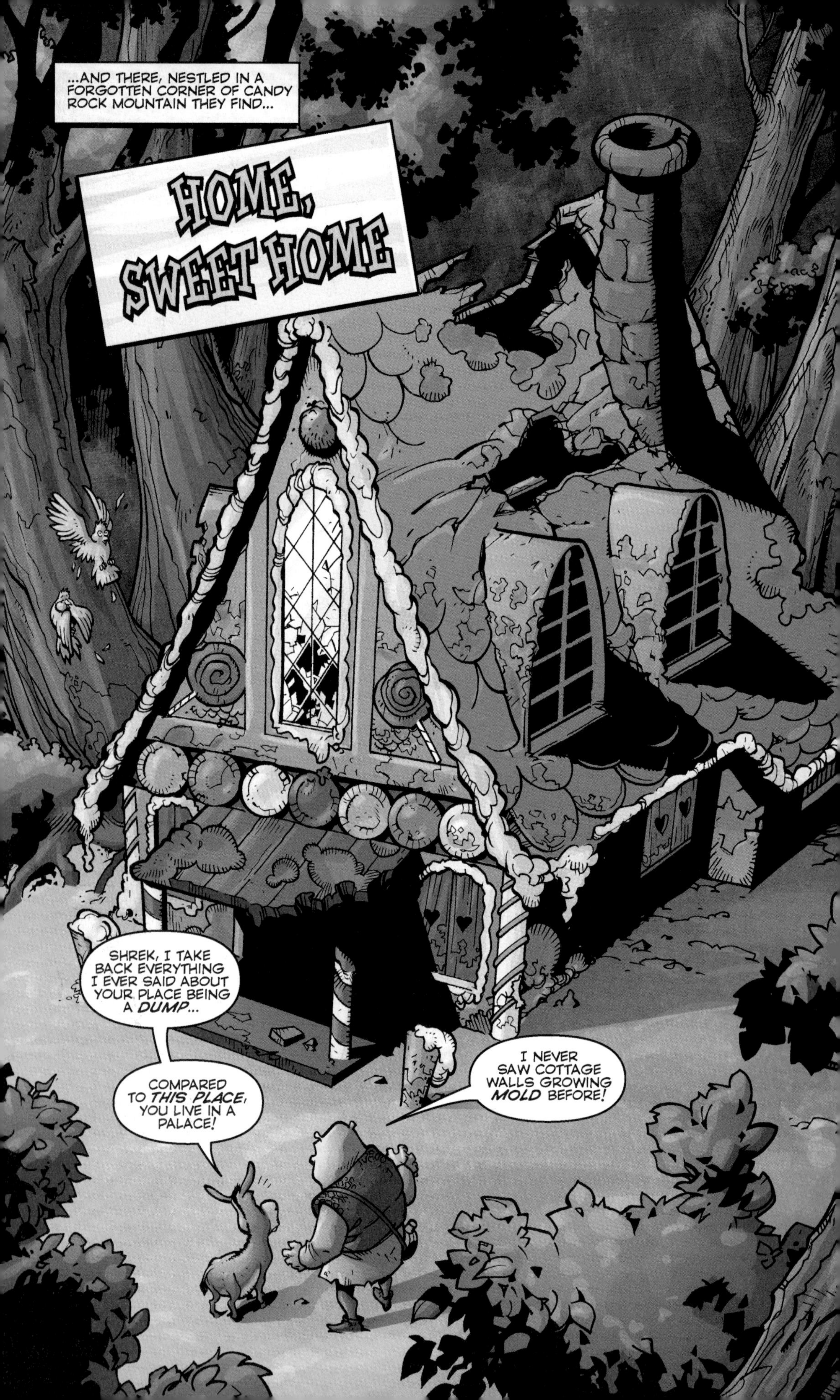
...AND THERE, NESTLED IN A FORGOTTEN CORNER OF CANDY ROCK MOUNTAIN THEY FIND...
HOME, SWEET HOME
SHREK, I TAKE BACK EVERYTHING I EVER SAID ABOUT YOUR PLACE BEING A DUMP...
COMPARED TO THIS PLACE, YOU LIVE IN A PALACE!
I NEVER SAW COTTAGE WALLS GROWING MOLD BEFORE!

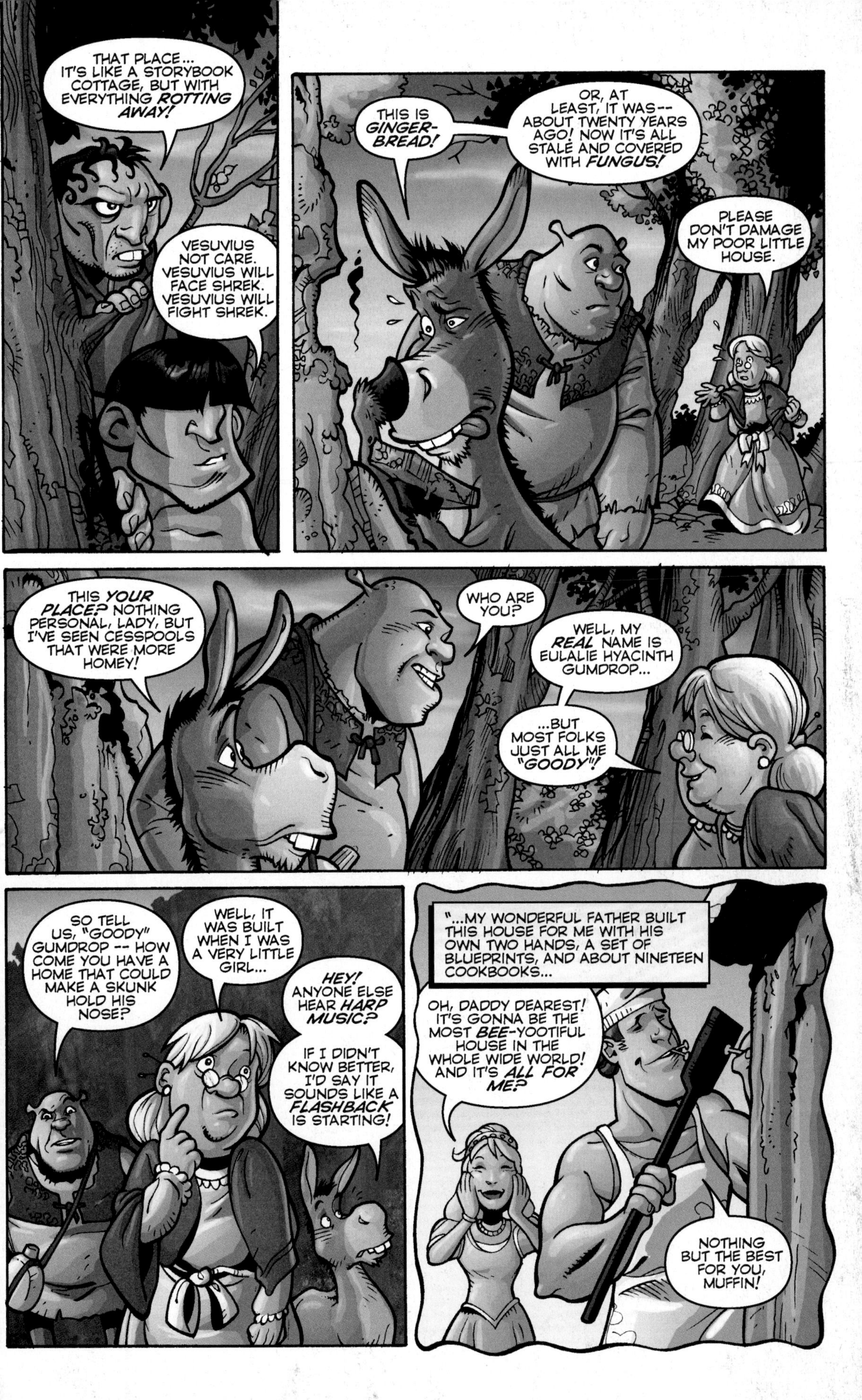
THAT PLACE... IT'S LIKE A STORYBOOK COTTAGE, BUT WITH EVERYTHING ROTTING AWAY!
VESUVIUS NOT CARE. VESUVIUS WILL FACE SHREK. VESUVIUS WILL FIGHT SHREK.
THIS IS GINGER-BREAD!
OR, AT LEAST, IT WAS-- ABOUT TWENTY YEARS AGO! NOW IT'S ALL STALE AND COVERED WITH FUNGUS!
PLEASE DON'T DAMAGE MY POOR LITTLE HOUSE.
THIS YOUR PLACE? NOTHING PERSONAL, LADY, BUT I'VE SEEN CESSPOOLS THAT WERE MORE HOMEY!
WHO ARE YOU?
WELL, MY REAL NAME IS EULALIE HYACINTH GUMDROP...
...BUT MOST FOLKS JUST ALL ME "GOODY"!
SO TELL US, "GOODY" GUMDROP -- HOW COME YOU HAVE A HOME THAT COULD MAKE A SKUNK HOLD HIS NOSE?
WELL, IT WAS BUILT WHEN I WAS A VERY LITTLE GIRL...
HEY! ANYONE ELSE HEAR HARP MUSIC?
IF I DIDN'T KNOW BETTER, I'D SAY IT SOUNDS LIKE A FLASHBACK IS STARTING!
"...MY WONDERFUL FATHER BUILT THIS HOUSE FOR ME WITH HIS OWN TWO HANDS, A SET OF BLUEPRINTS, AND ABOUT NINETEEN COOKBOOKS...
OH, DADDY DEAREST! IT'S GONNA BE THE MOST BEE-YOOTIFUL HOUSE IN THE WHOLE WIDE WORLD! AND IT'S ALL FOR ME?
NOTHING BUT THE BEST FOR YOU, MUFFIN!

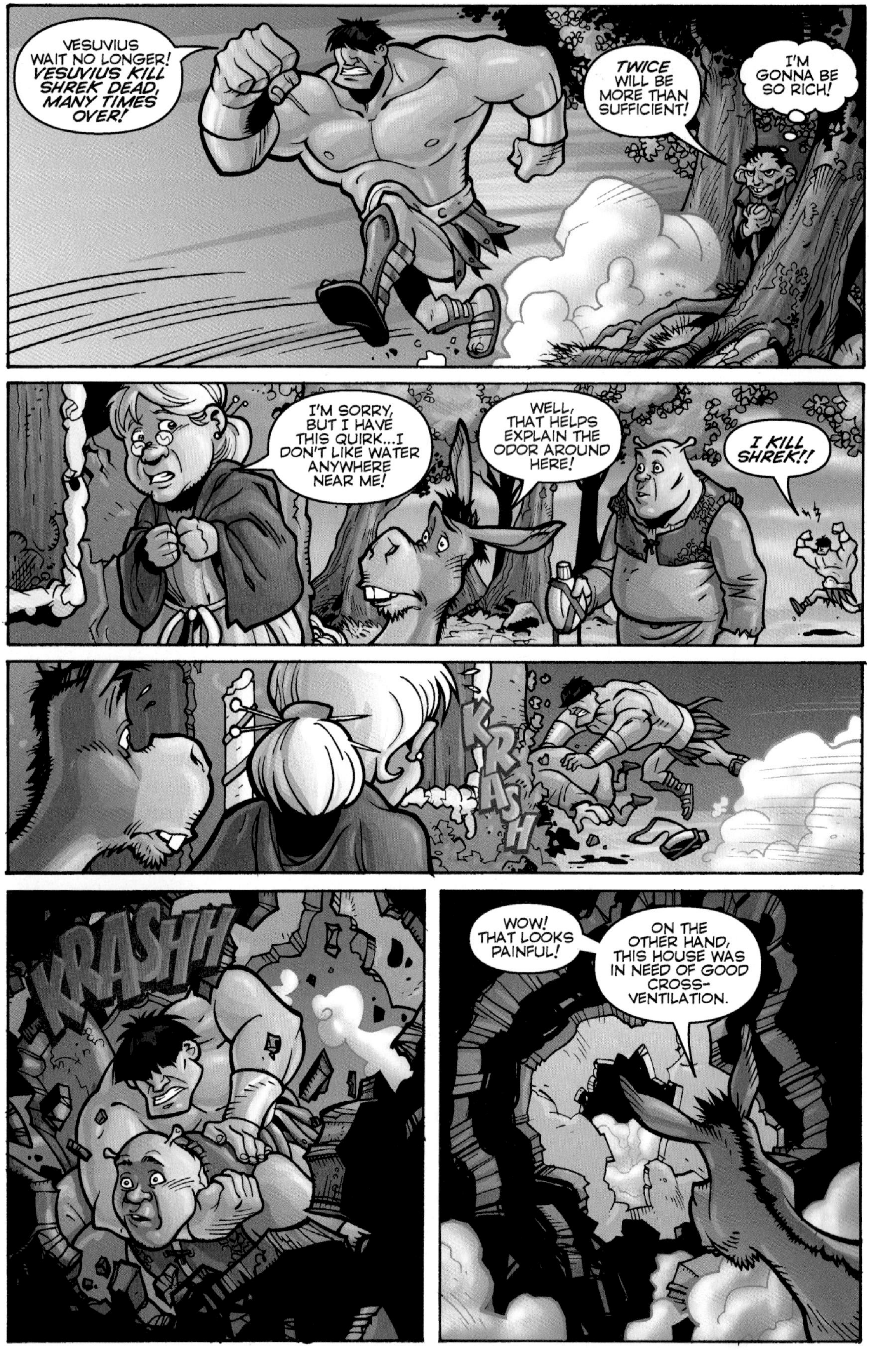
VESUVIUS WAIT NO LONGER! VESUVIUS KILL SHREK DEAD, MANY TIMES OVER!
TWICE WILL BE MORE THAN SUFFICIENT!
I'M GONNA BE SO RICH!
I'M SORRY, BUT I HAVE THIS QUIRK...I DON'T LIKE WATER ANYWHERE NEAR ME!
WELL, THAT HELPS EXPLAIN THE ODOR AROUND HERE!
I KILL SHREK!!
KRASH
KRASHH
WOW! THAT LOOKS PAINFUL!
ON THE OTHER HAND, THIS HOUSE WAS IN NEED OF GOOD CROSS-VENTILATION.

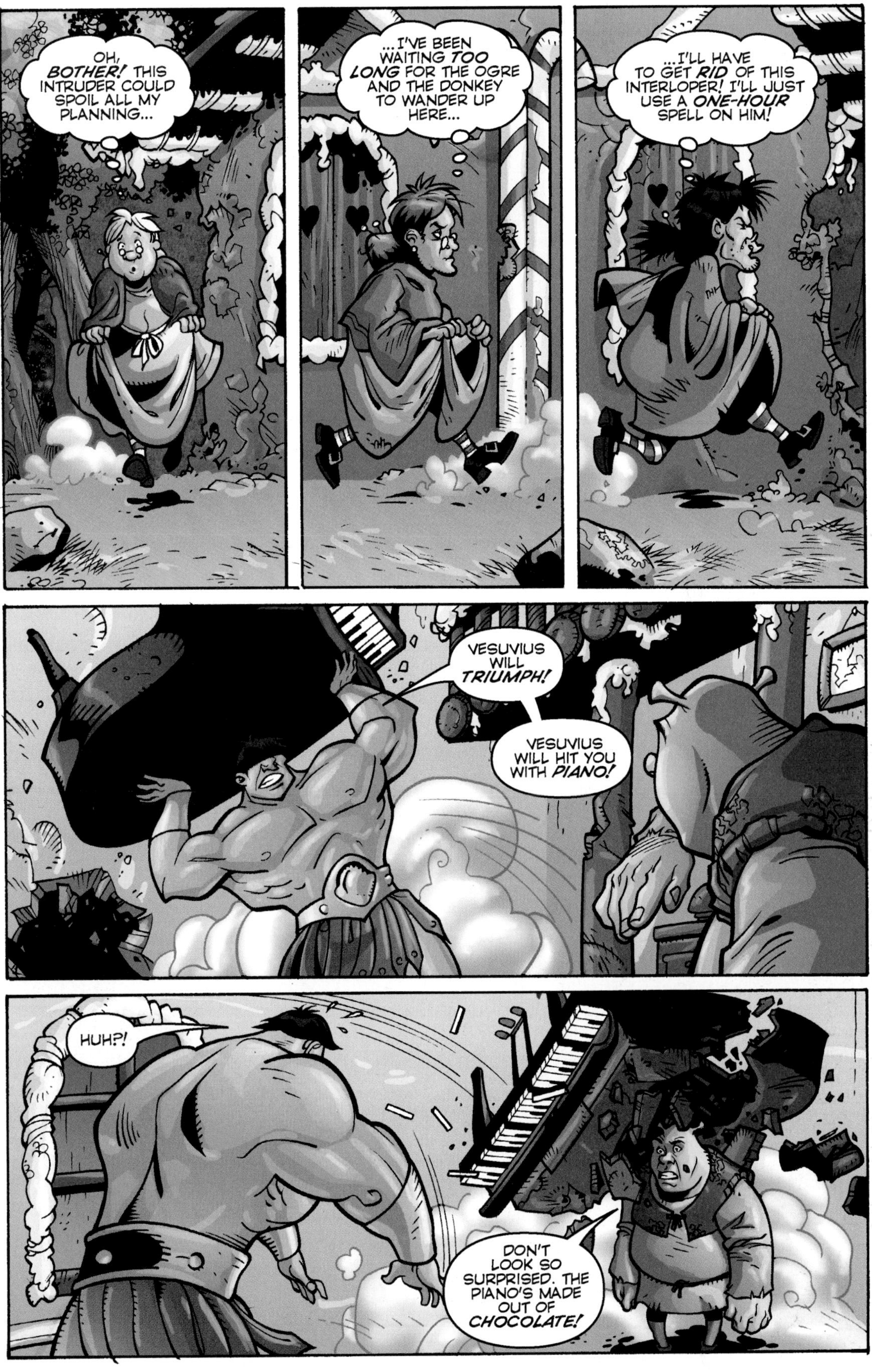
OH, BOTHER! THIS INTRUDER COULD SPOIL ALL MY PLANNING...
...I'VE BEEN WAITING TOO LONG FOR THE OGRE AND THE DONKEY TO WANDER UP HERE...
...I'LL HAVE TO GET RID OF THIS INTERLOPER! I'LL JUST USE A ONE-HOUR SPELL ON HIM!
VESUVIUS WILL TRIUMPH!
VESUVIUS WILL HIT YOU WITH PIANO!
HUH?!
DON'T LOOK SO SURPRISED. THE PIANO'S MADE OUT OF CHOCOLATE!

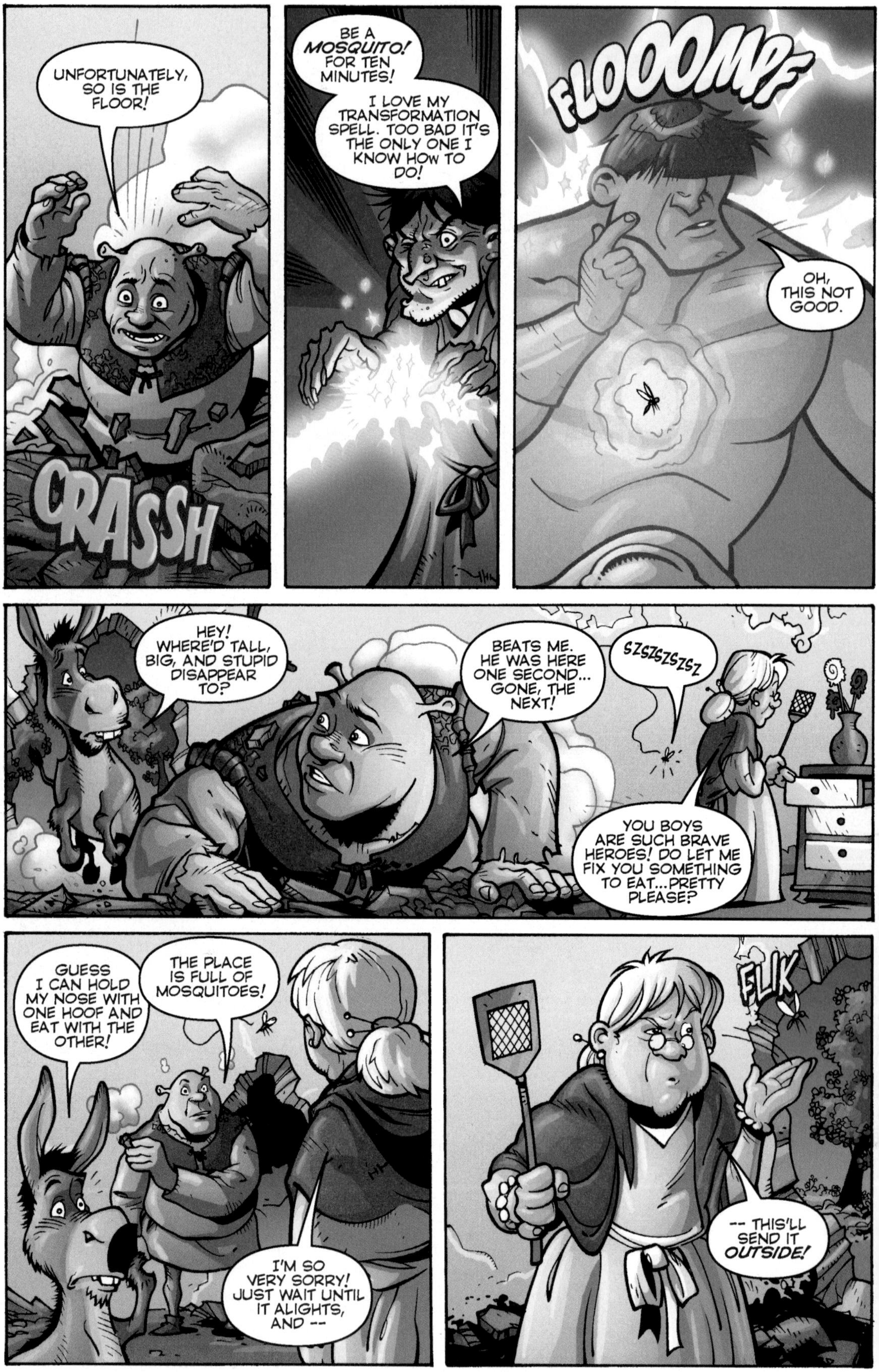

UNFORTUNATELY, SO IS THE FLOOR!
CRASSH
BE A MOSQUITO! FOR TEN MINUTES!
I LOVE MY TRANSFORMATION SPELL. TOO BAD IT'S THE ONLY ONE I KNOW HOW TO DO!
FLOOOMPF
OH, THIS NOT GOOD.
HEY! WHERE'D TALL, BIG, AND STUPID DISAPPEAR TO?
BEATS ME. HE WAS HERE ONE SECOND... GONE, THE NEXT!
SZSZSZSZSZ
YOU BOYS ARE SUCH BRAVE HEROES! DO LET ME FIX YOU SOMETHING TO EAT...PRETTY PLEASE?
GUESS I CAN HOLD MY NOSE WITH ONE HOOF AND EAT WITH THE OTHER!
THE PLACE IS FULL OF MOSQUITOES!
I'M SO VERY SORRY! JUST WAIT UNTIL IT ALIGHTS, AND --
FLIK
-- THIS'LL SEND IT OUTSIDE!

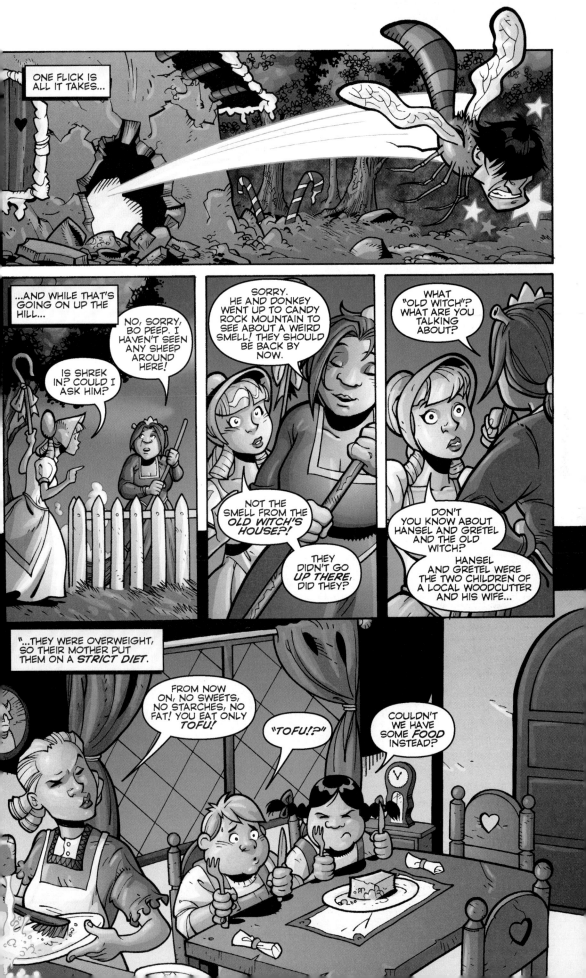

OUTSIDE THE WITCH'S COTTAGE ARE TWO INSECTS -- FERRET AND A MOSQUITO...

SZSZSZSZSZSZ

I NEED VESUVIUS TO HELP ME GET RID OF SHREK! WHERE DID THAT IDIOT DISAPPEAR TO?

FLO OMP

SHE TURNED ME INTO A MOSQUITO, FERRET! SHE DID! SHE REALLY DID!

GET... OFF... ME.

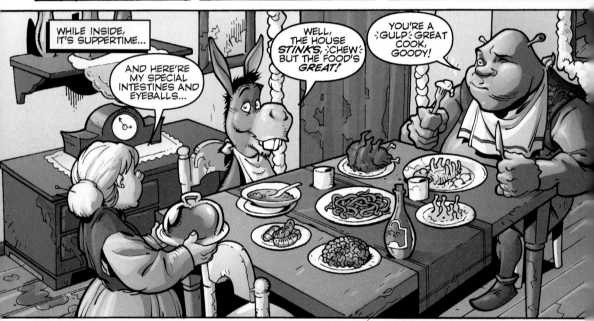

WHILE INSIDE, IT'S SUPPERTIME...

AND HERE'RE MY SPECIAL INTESTINES AND EYEBALLS...

WELL, THE HOUSE STINKS, CHEW BUT THE FOOD'S GREAT!

YOU'RE A GULP GREAT COOK, GOODY!

OH, THANK YOU. I DON'T GET MUCH COMPANY HERE.

CONSIDERING THE SMELL, THAT'S NOT GULP HARD TO EXPLAIN.

DONKEY-OGRE STEW

1 DONKEY (MEDIUM-SIZED)
1 OGRE (PREFERABLY GREEN)
5 CUPS FESTERING YAK BROTH
1 CUP GILA MONSTERS (FINELY CHOPPED)
1/2 CUP PAPRIKA
COMBINE INGREDIENTS IN LARGE
CAULDRON AND SIMMER OVER OPEN
FLAME. ADD EYE OF NEWT TO TASTE.

I THOUGHT YOU SAID YOU KNEW WHERE IT WAS!

IT'S *THIS WAY*, I THINK...

...OR IS IT *THAT* WAY?

OH, I GET SO *CONFUSED!* NO WONDER I KEEP LOSING MY SHEEP!

AH-CHOO!

FIONA! I WAS GOING TO FIND HELP, AND YOU'RE IT! *COME ON!*

DONKEY! IS THAT *YOU?* HOW DID YOU BECOME A *CAT?*

AND, BY THE WAY -- *GESUNDHEIT!*

SAME WAY YOU BECAME AN *OGRE* AFTER ALL THOSE YEARS AS A SUPERMODEL -- ONE OF THOSE MAGIC SPELL THINGIES!

HURRY! BEFORE SHREK BECOMES THE SOUP OF THE DAY!

BO PEEP! YOU CIRCLE AROUND THE BACK! I'LL FOLLOW CAT!

I MEAN, *DONKEY!*

WE'RE GOING TO TAKE HIM TO LORD FARQUAAD!

YEAH! HOW DO YOU THINK YOU'RE GONNA *STOP US?*

GET AWAY FROM MY DINNER!

LIKE *THIS --!*

YOU TWO! *BE SHEEP!* FOREVER!

I DON'T THINK ASKING HER THAT WAS A VERY SMART MOVE!

FLOOMP

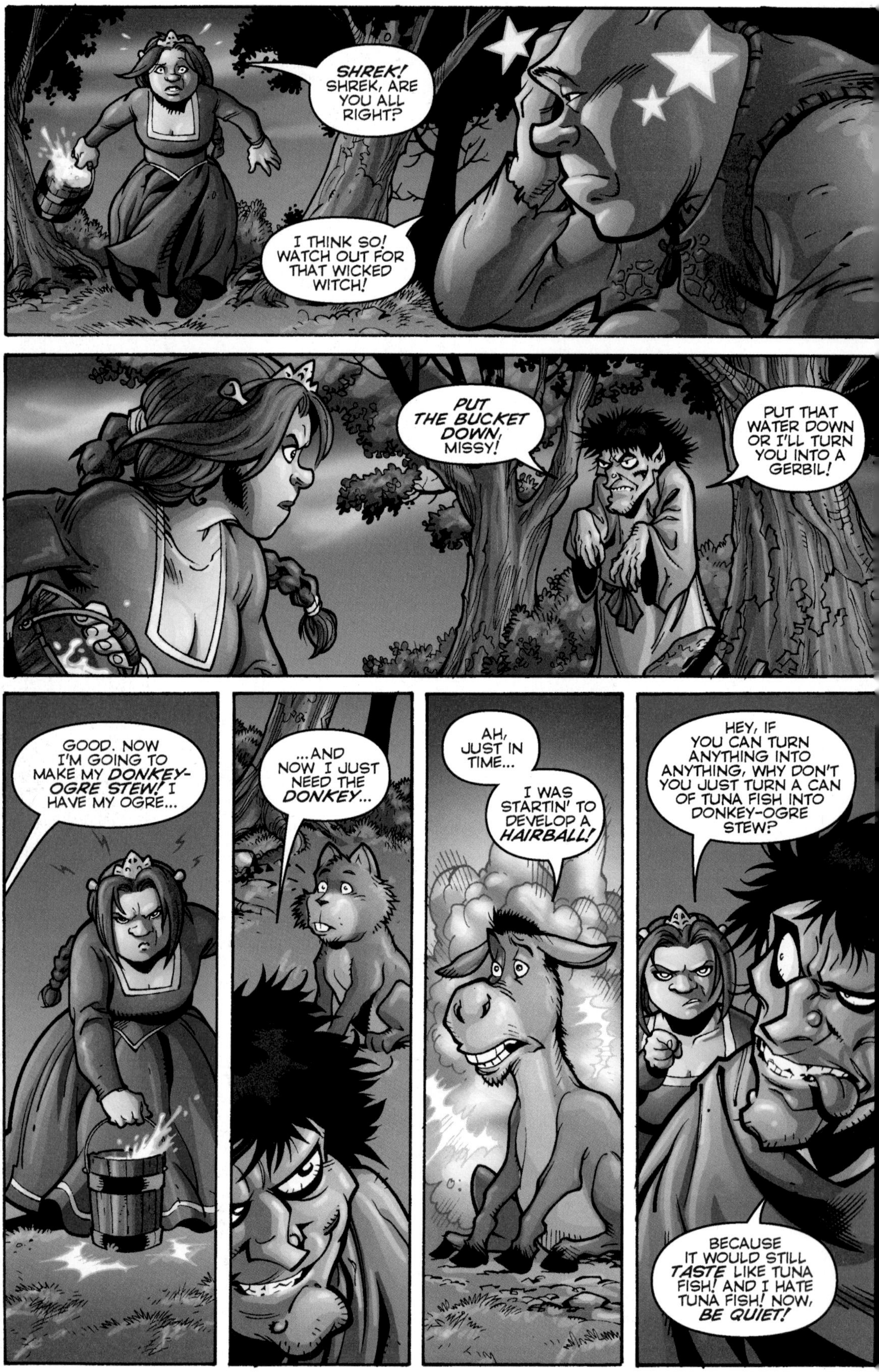
SHREK! SHREK, ARE YOU ALL RIGHT?
I THINK SO! WATCH OUT FOR THAT WICKED WITCH!
PUT THE BUCKET DOWN, MISSY!
PUT THAT WATER DOWN OR I'LL TURN YOU INTO A GERBIL!
GOOD. NOW I'M GOING TO MAKE MY DONKEY-OGRE STEW! I HAVE MY OGRE...
...AND NOW I JUST NEED THE DONKEY...
AH, JUST IN TIME...
I WAS STARTIN' TO DEVELOP A HAIRBALL!
HEY, IF YOU CAN TURN ANYTHING INTO ANYTHING, WHY DON'T YOU JUST TURN A CAN OF TUNA FISH INTO DONKEY-OGRE STEW?
BECAUSE IT WOULD STILL TASTE LIKE TUNA FISH! AND I HATE TUNA FISH! NOW, BE QUIET!

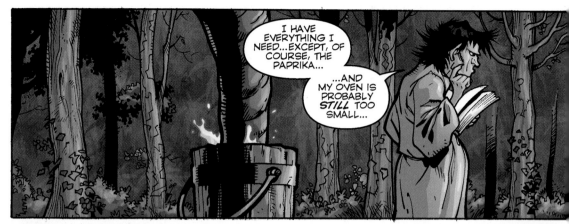

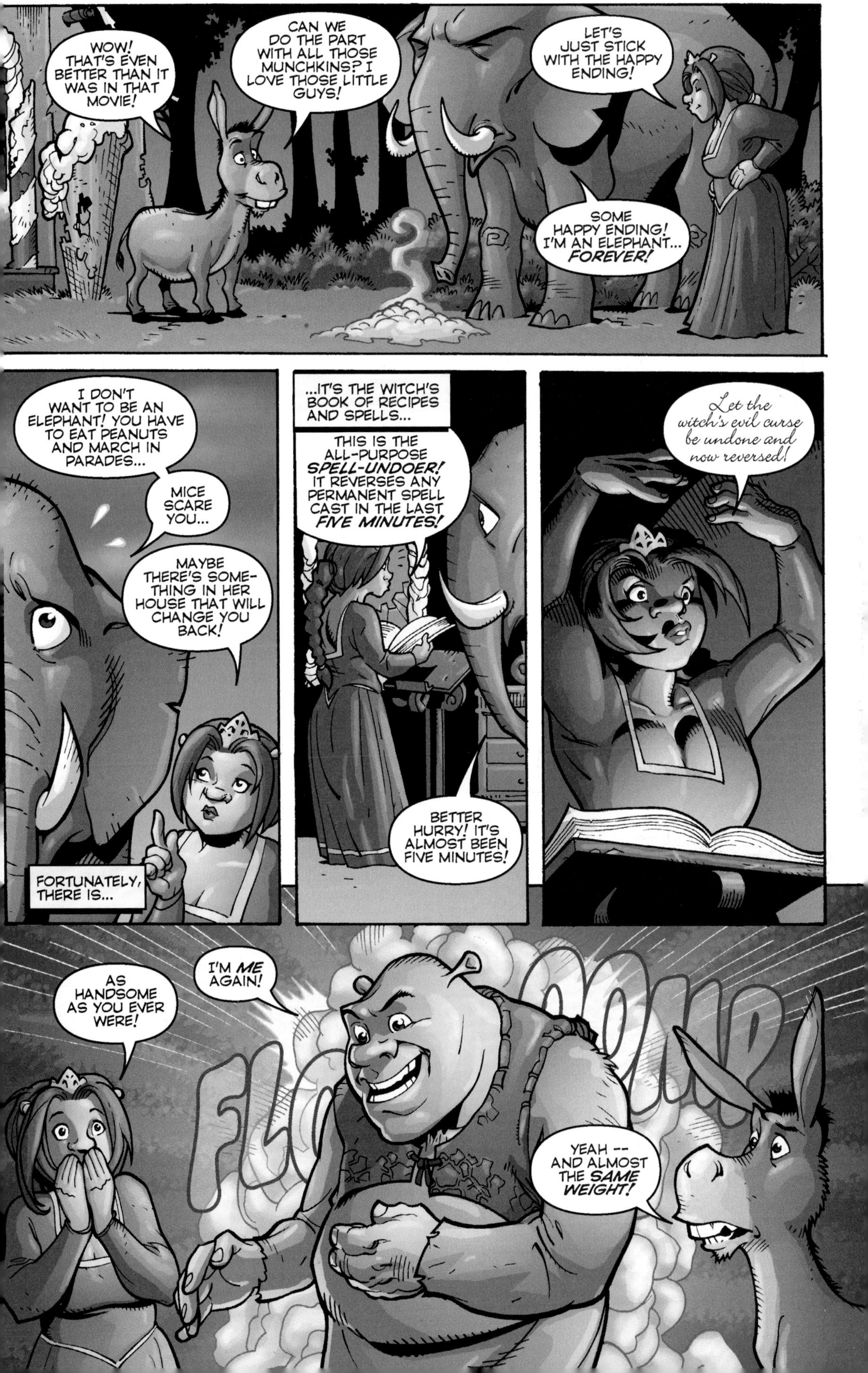
WOW! THAT'S EVEN BETTER THAN IT WAS IN THAT MOVIE!
CAN WE DO THE PART WITH ALL THOSE MUNCHKINS? I LOVE THOSE LITTLE GUYS!
LET'S JUST STICK WITH THE HAPPY ENDING!
SOME HAPPY ENDING! I'M AN ELEPHANT... FOREVER!
I DON'T WANT TO BE AN ELEPHANT! YOU HAVE TO EAT PEANUTS AND MARCH IN PARADES...
MICE SCARE YOU...
MAYBE THERE'S SOMETHING IN HER HOUSE THAT WILL CHANGE YOU BACK!
FORTUNATELY, THERE IS...
...IT'S THE WITCH'S BOOK OF RECIPES AND SPELLS...
THIS IS THE ALL-PURPOSE SPELL-UNDOER! IT REVERSES ANY PERMANENT SPELL CAST IN THE LAST FIVE MINUTES!
BETTER HURRY! IT'S ALMOST BEEN FIVE MINUTES!
Let the witch's evil curse be undone and now reversed!
AS HANDSOME AS YOU EVER WERE!
I'M ME AGAIN!
YEAH -- AND ALMOST THE SAME WEIGHT!

THE END

"RIVER"?! DID I SAY "RIVER"?

YES, I DID! I DISTINCTLY HEARD MYSELF JUST SAY "RIVER"!

AND LOOK AT THAT! THEY'RE GOING BED-CANOEING AND DIDN'T HAVE THE DECENCY TO INVITE ME!

SHREK! ARE YOU SURE WE AREN'T DREAMING?

BOTH OF US? HAVING THE SAME DREAM AT THE SAME TIME? NOT LIKELY!

THERE WAS NO RIVER HERE LAST NIGHT WHEN I LEFT SHREK'S HOUSE!

ANY IDEA WHY WE WOKE UP ROLLIN' ON THE RIVER?

NOT A CLUE!

IS THAT WHAT THEY CALL A RIVER BED?

SORRY... COULDN'T RESIST...

COME ON, DONKEY! LET'S GO UPSTREAM AND FIND OUT WHY MY HOME IS NOW DOWNSTREAM!

YOU CAN'T GO RUNNING AROUND IN YOUR PJ'S, SHREK-- AND YOUR CLOTHES ARE ALL BACK IN THE HOUSE, UNDERWATER!

DON'T WORRY! HERE COMES MY SPRING WARDROBE... FLOATING ALONG ON THE SPRING!

AS SOON AS I GET DRESSED, WE'LL GET TO THE SOURCE!

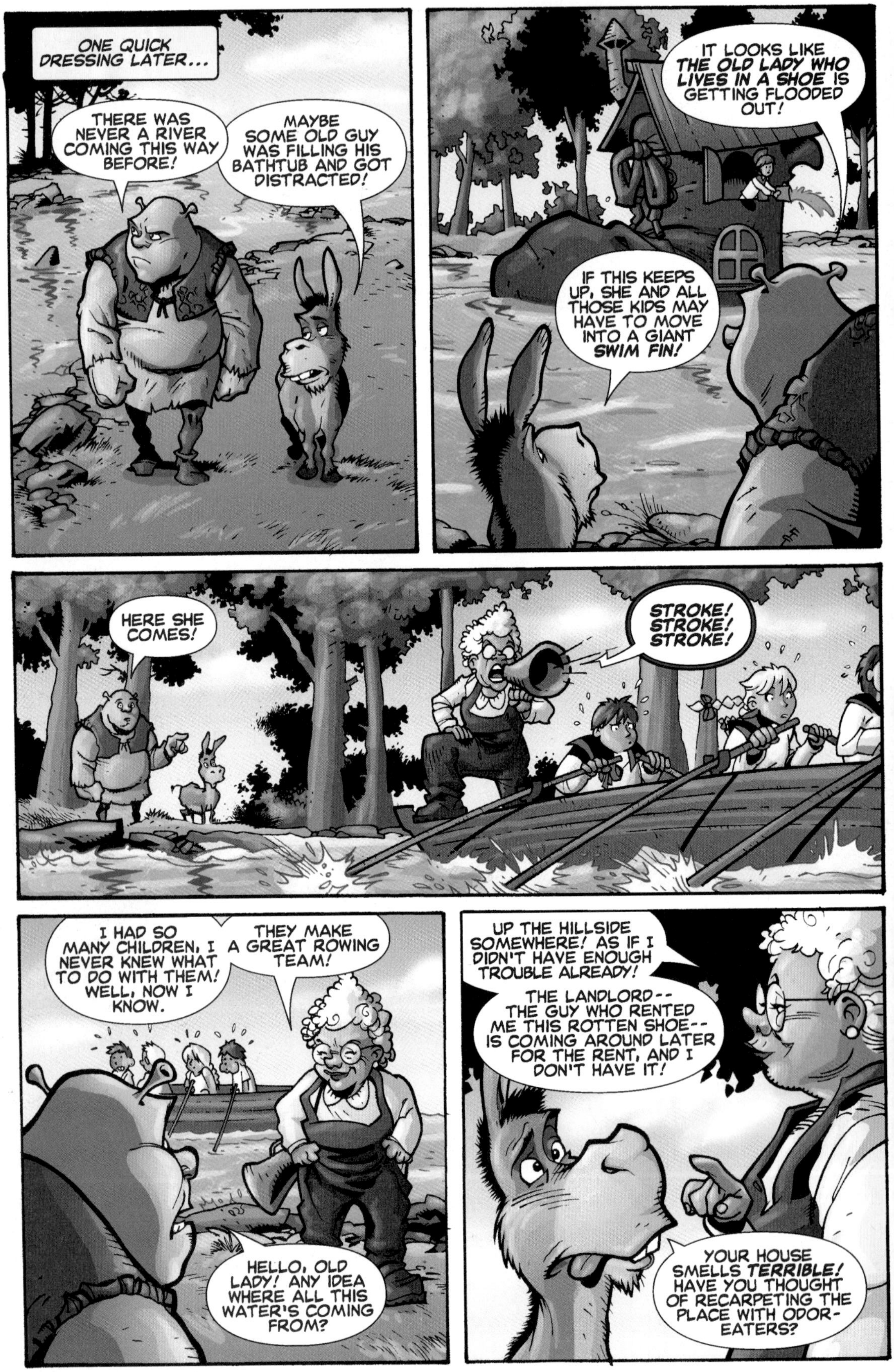
ONE QUICK DRESSING LATER...
THERE WAS NEVER A RIVER COMING THIS WAY BEFORE!
MAYBE SOME OLD GUY WAS FILLING HIS BATHTUB AND GOT DISTRACTED!
IT LOOKS LIKE THE OLD LADY WHO LIVES IN A SHOE IS GETTING FLOODED OUT!
IF THIS KEEPS UP, SHE AND ALL THOSE KIDS MAY HAVE TO MOVE INTO A GIANT SWIM FIN!
HERE SHE COMES!
STROKE! STROKE! STROKE!
I HAD SO MANY CHILDREN, I NEVER KNEW WHAT TO DO WITH THEM! WELL, NOW I KNOW.
THEY MAKE A GREAT ROWING TEAM!
HELLO, OLD LADY! ANY IDEA WHERE ALL THIS WATER'S COMING FROM?
UP THE HILLSIDE SOMEWHERE! AS IF I DIDN'T HAVE ENOUGH TROUBLE ALREADY!
THE LANDLORD--THE GUY WHO RENTED ME THIS ROTTEN SHOE--IS COMING AROUND LATER FOR THE RENT, AND I DON'T HAVE IT!
YOUR HOUSE SMELLS TERRIBLE! HAVE YOU THOUGHT OF RECARPETING THE PLACE WITH ODOR-EATERS?

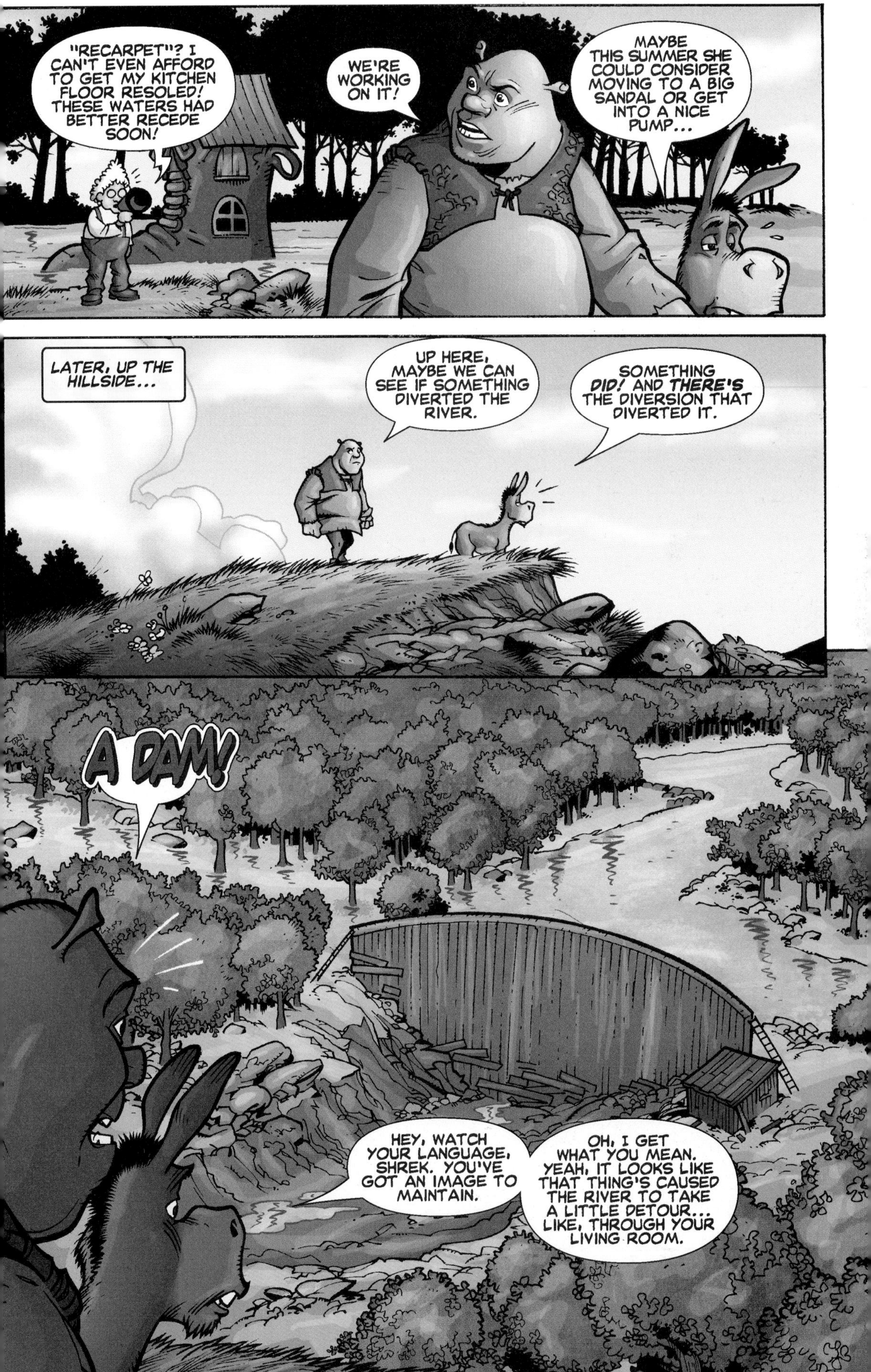
"RECARPET"? I CAN'T EVEN AFFORD TO GET MY KITCHEN FLOOR RESOLED! THESE WATERS HAD BETTER RECEDE SOON!
WE'RE WORKING ON IT!
MAYBE THIS SUMMER SHE COULD CONSIDER MOVING TO A BIG SANDAL OR GET INTO A NICE PUMP...
LATER, UP THE HILLSIDE...
UP HERE, MAYBE WE CAN SEE IF SOMETHING DIVERTED THE RIVER.
SOMETHING *DID!* AND ***THERE'S*** THE DIVERSION THAT DIVERTED IT.
A DAM!
HEY, WATCH YOUR LANGUAGE, SHREK. YOU'VE GOT AN IMAGE TO MAINTAIN.
OH, I GET WHAT YOU MEAN. YEAH, IT LOOKS LIKE THAT THING'S CAUSED THE RIVER TO TAKE A LITTLE DETOUR... LIKE, THROUGH YOUR LIVING ROOM.

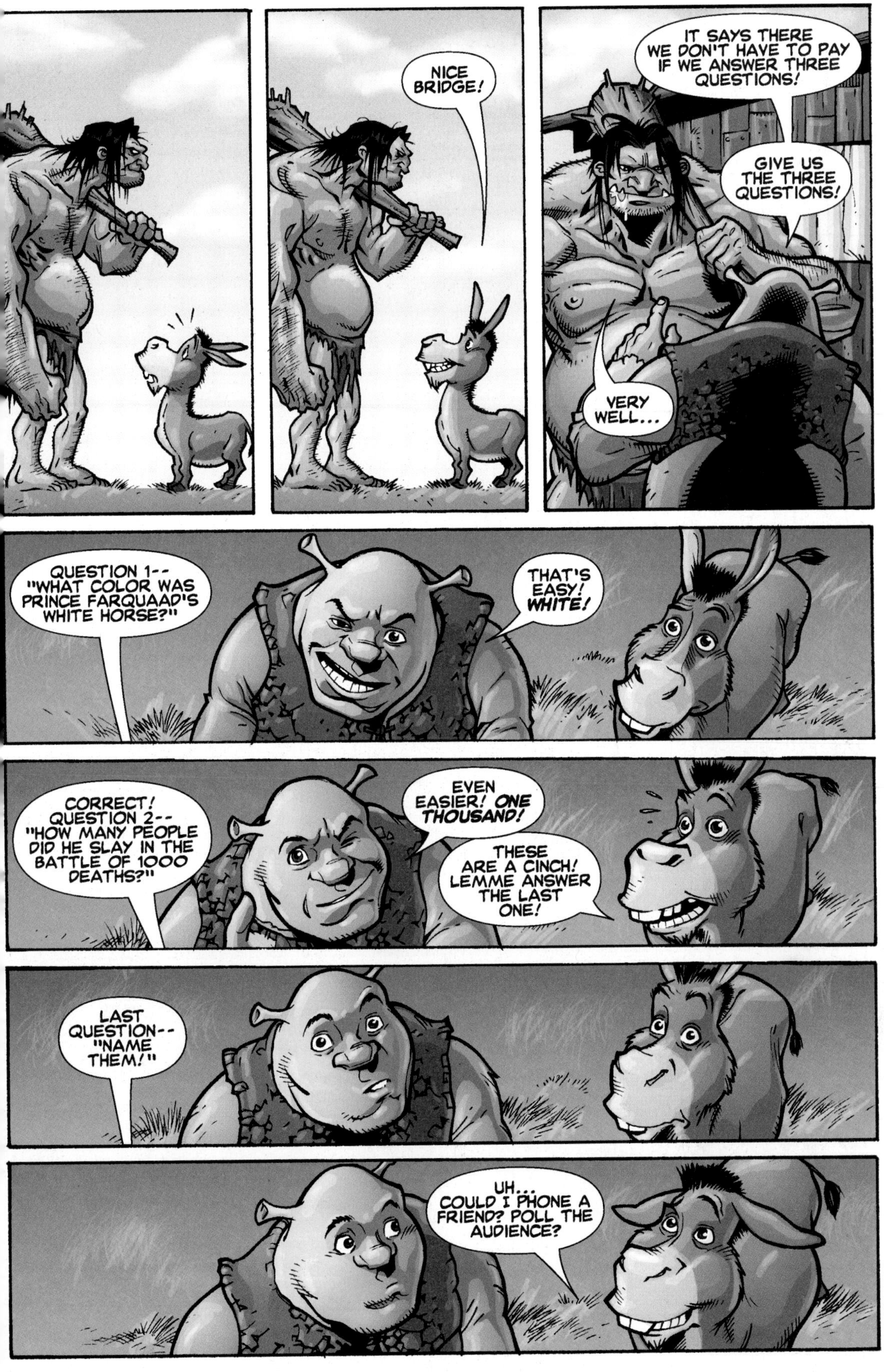
NICE BRIDGE!
IT SAYS THERE WE DON'T HAVE TO PAY IF WE ANSWER THREE QUESTIONS!
GIVE US THE THREE QUESTIONS!
VERY WELL...
QUESTION 1-- "WHAT COLOR WAS PRINCE FARQUAAD'S WHITE HORSE?"
THAT'S EASY! WHITE!
CORRECT! QUESTION 2-- "HOW MANY PEOPLE DID HE SLAY IN THE BATTLE OF 1000 DEATHS?"
EVEN EASIER! ONE THOUSAND!
THESE ARE A CINCH! LEMME ANSWER THE LAST ONE!
LAST QUESTION-- "NAME THEM!"
UH... COULD I PHONE A FRIEND? POLL THE AUDIENCE?

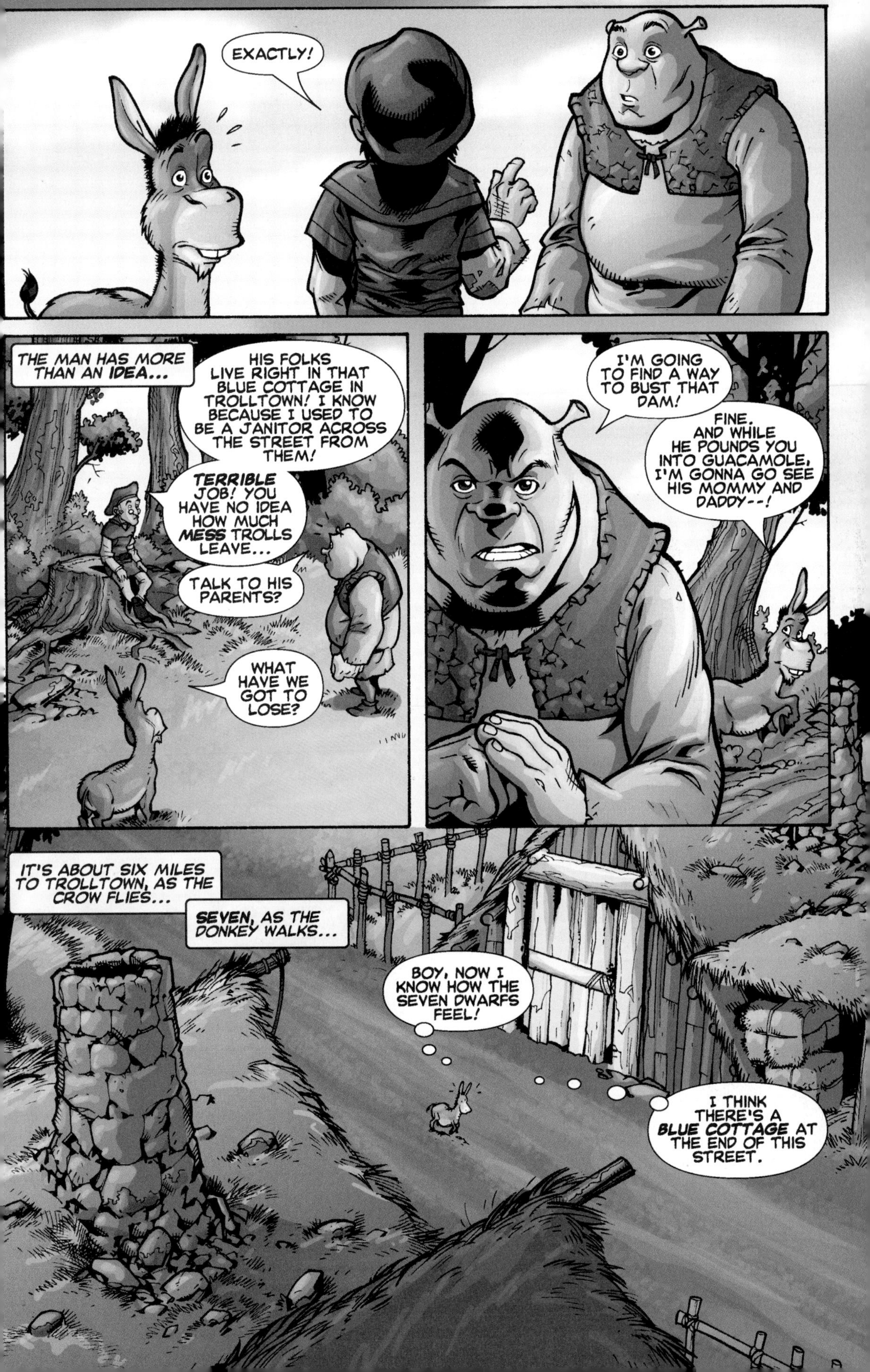
EXACTLY!
THE MAN HAS MORE THAN AN IDEA...
HIS FOLKS LIVE RIGHT IN THAT BLUE COTTAGE IN TROLLTOWN! I KNOW BECAUSE I USED TO BE A JANITOR ACROSS THE STREET FROM THEM!
TERRIBLE JOB! YOU HAVE NO IDEA HOW MUCH MESS TROLLS LEAVE...
TALK TO HIS PARENTS?
WHAT HAVE WE GOT TO LOSE?
I'M GOING TO FIND A WAY TO BUST THAT DAM!
FINE. AND WHILE HE POUNDS YOU INTO GUACAMOLE, I'M GONNA GO SEE HIS MOMMY AND DADDY--!
IT'S ABOUT SIX MILES TO TROLLTOWN, AS THE CROW FLIES...
SEVEN, AS THE DONKEY WALKS...
BOY, NOW I KNOW HOW THE SEVEN DWARFS FEEL!
I THINK THERE'S A BLUE COTTAGE AT THE END OF THIS STREET.

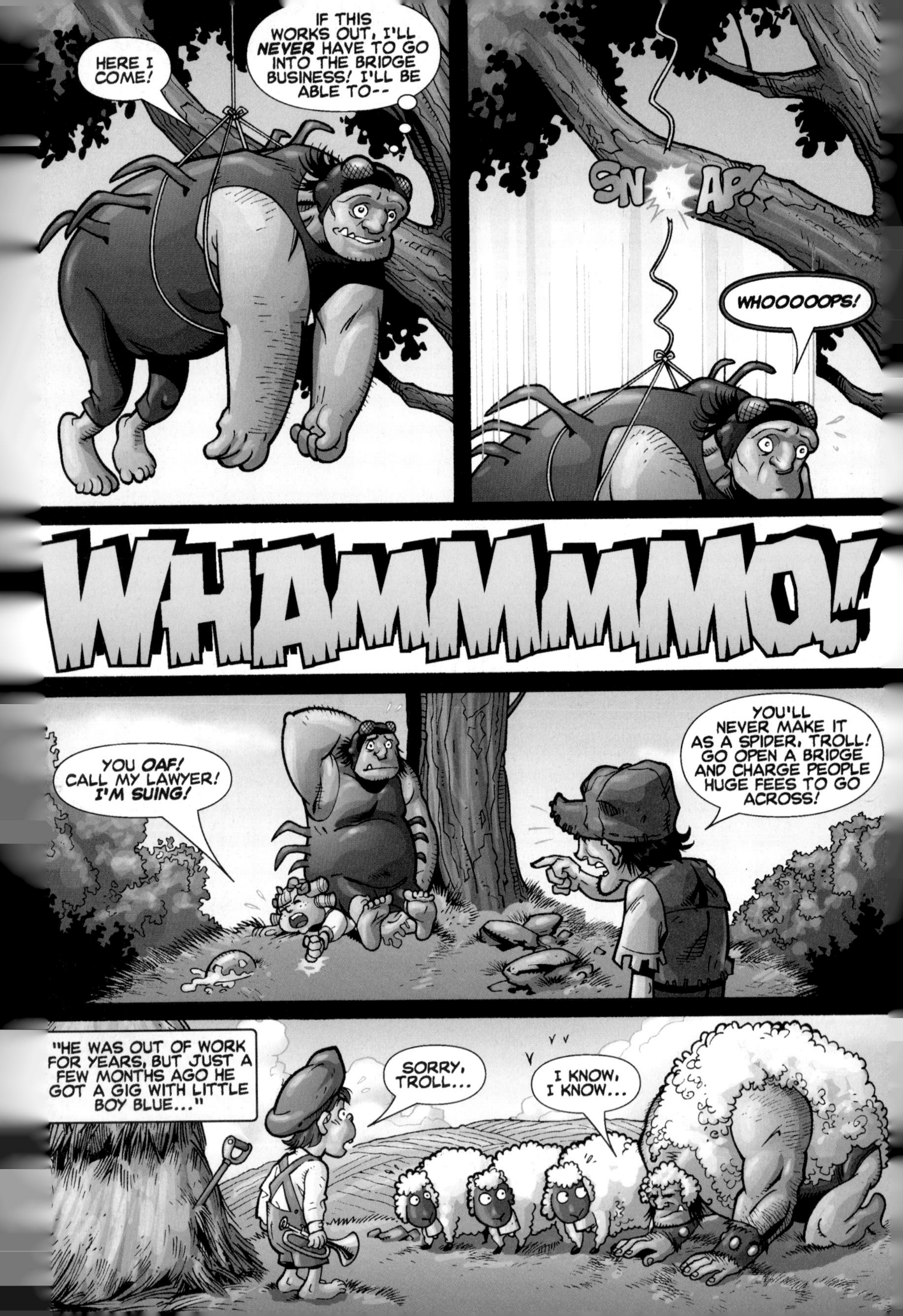
HERE I COME!
IF THIS WORKS OUT, I'LL NEVER HAVE TO GO INTO THE BRIDGE BUSINESS! I'LL BE ABLE TO--
SN AP!
WHOOOOOPS!
WHAMMMMMO!
YOU OAF! CALL MY LAWYER! I'M SUING!
YOU'LL NEVER MAKE IT AS A SPIDER, TROLL! GO OPEN A BRIDGE AND CHARGE PEOPLE HUGE FEES TO GO ACROSS!
"HE WAS OUT OF WORK FOR YEARS, BUT JUST A FEW MONTHS AGO HE GOT A GIG WITH LITTLE BOY BLUE..."
SORRY, TROLL...
I KNOW, I KNOW...

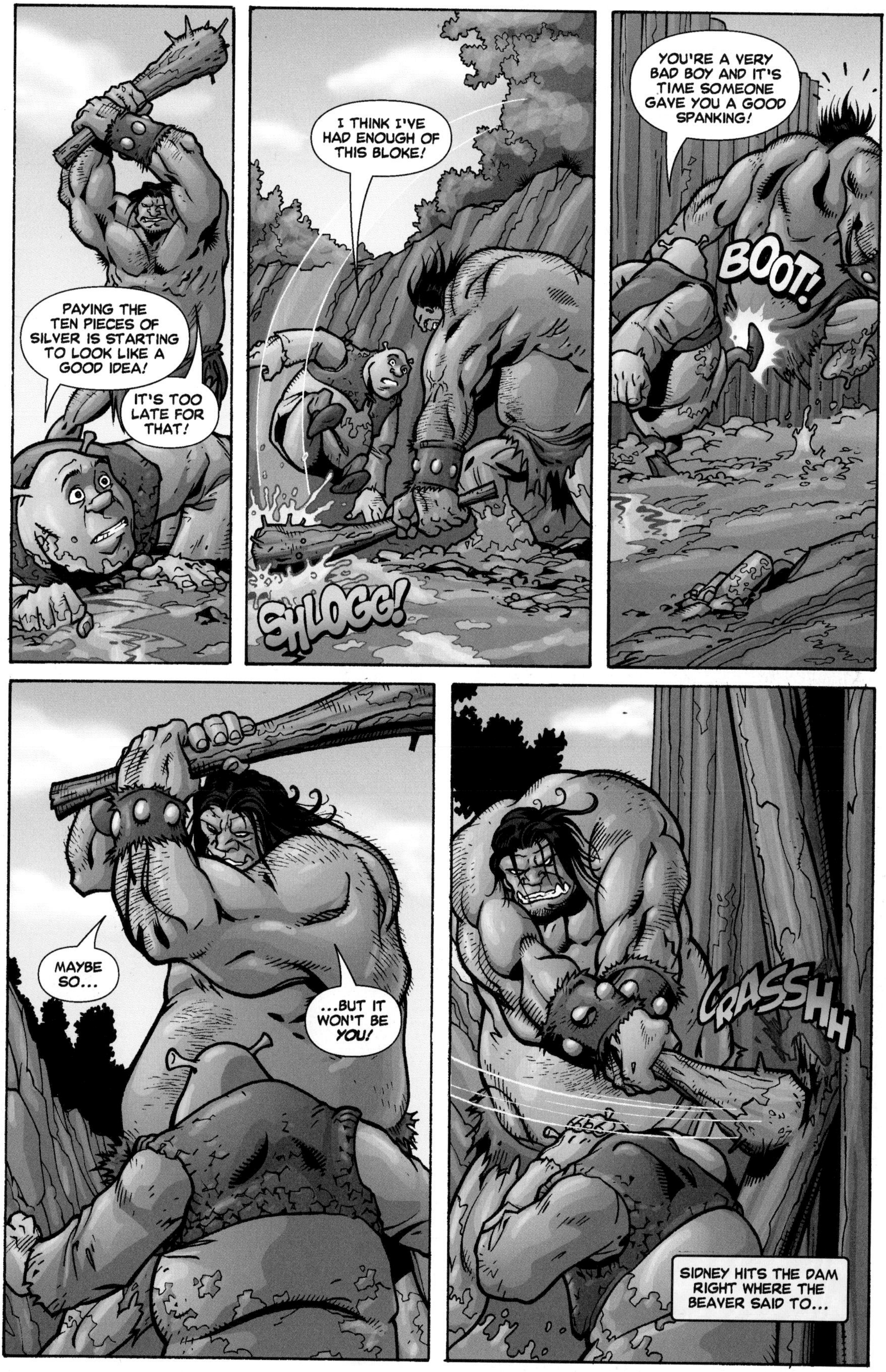
PAYING THE TEN PIECES OF SILVER IS STARTING TO LOOK LIKE A GOOD IDEA!
IT'S TOO LATE FOR THAT!
I THINK I'VE HAD ENOUGH OF THIS BLOKE!
SHLOGG!
YOU'RE A VERY BAD BOY AND IT'S TIME SOMEONE GAVE YOU A GOOD SPANKING!
BOOT!
MAYBE SO...
...BUT IT WON'T BE YOU!
CRASSHH
SIDNEY HITS THE DAM RIGHT WHERE THE BEAVER SAID TO...

THE RIVER'S GOING BACK THE WAY IT WAS!

PRETTY SOON, EVERYTHING THAT FLOODED...INCLUDING MY LIVING ROOM... WILL DRY OUT!

SO WHAT? I'LL JUST BUILD *ANOTHER* DAM!

I'M A TROLL AND THAT'S WHAT TROLLS DO! THAT'S ALL ANYONE *EVER* WANTS US TO DO!

BUZZ BUZZ BUZZ! WHISPER WHISPER WHISPER!

YOU *MEAN* IT? YOU'RE NOT KIDDING ME, ARE YOU?

MAYBE NOT! LIFT ME UP TO EAR-LEVEL, FELLA! I GOT A PROPOSITION FOR YOU!

I *NEVER* KID! I FIB, I LIE, I UTTER UNTRUTHFUL STATE-MENTS...BUT I *NEVER* KID!

COME ON! FOLLOW ME...AND I'LL MAKE YOUR DREAM COME TRUE!

AND SO...

OLD LADY! OLD LADY WHO LIVES IN THIS SHOE, *OPEN THE DOOR!*

THIS IS YOUR *LANDLORD!* I KNOW YOU'RE IN THERE! I'VE COME FOR THE RENT!

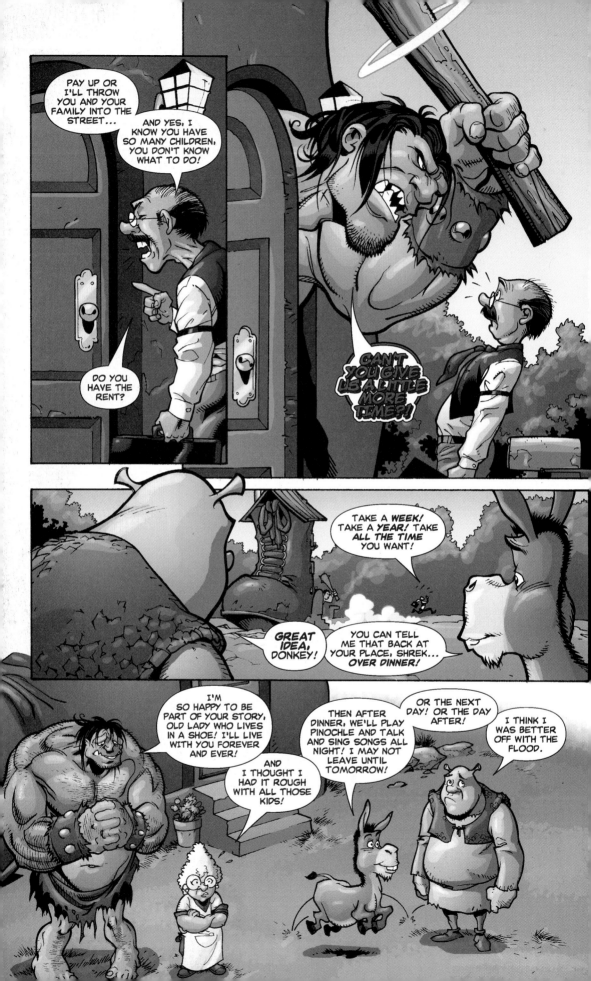

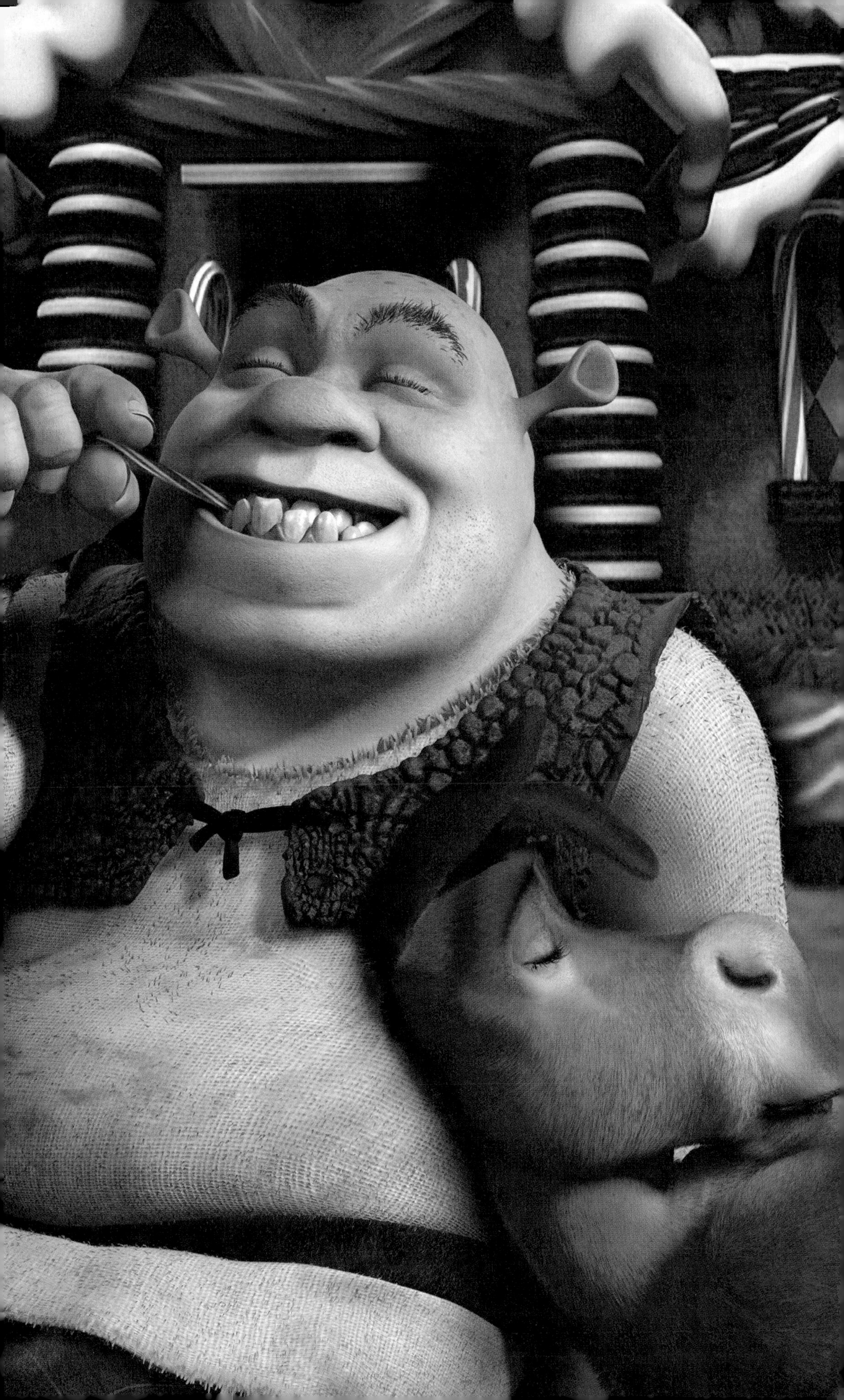

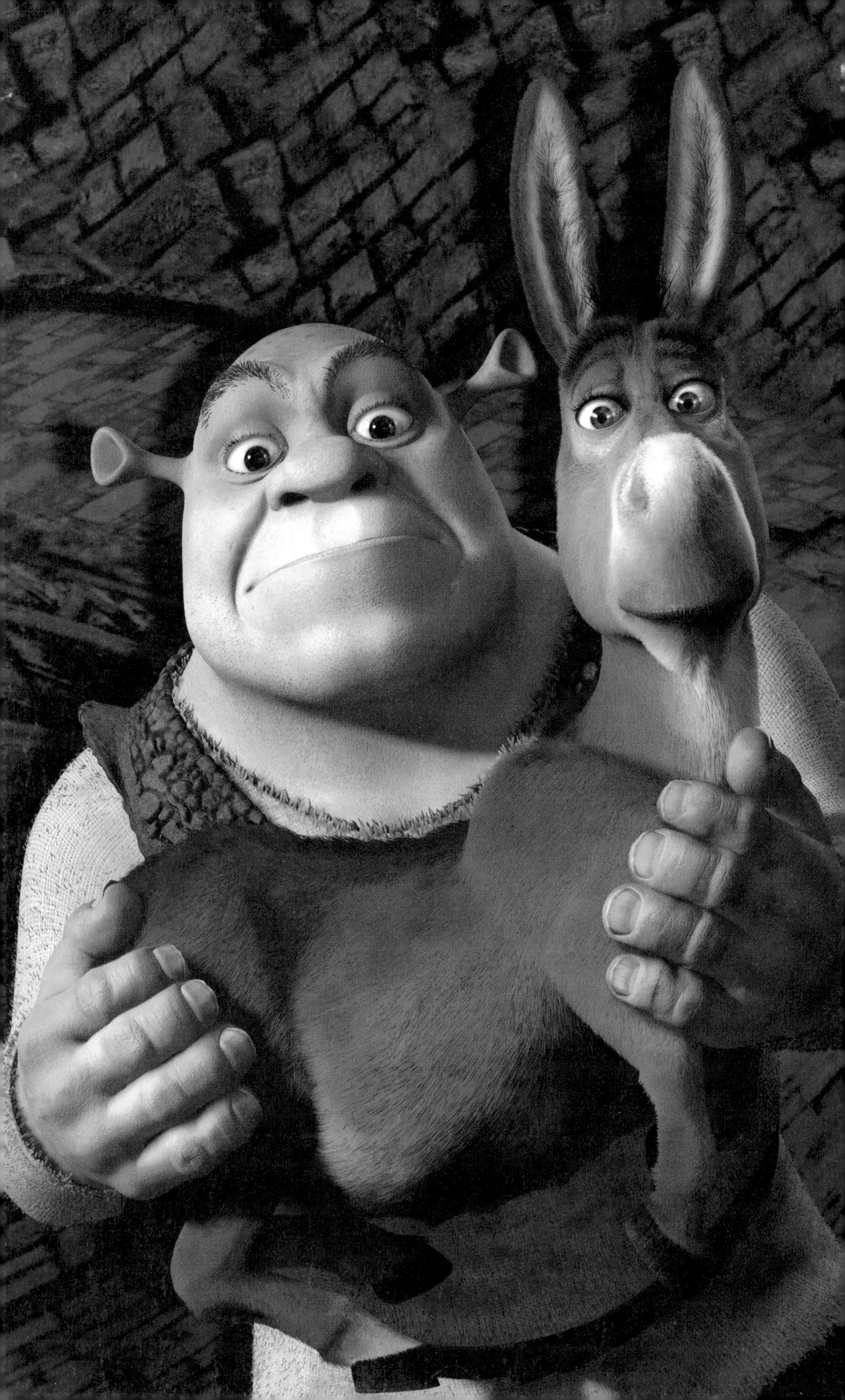